FIGHTING FOR YOUR DREAM

MASTERING RESILIENCE
AND PERFORMING
WHEN IT REALLY MATTERS

Fighting for Your Dream:
Mastering resilience and performing when it really matters

Every possible effort has been made to ensure that the information contained in this publication is accurate at the time of going to press. Neither the publisher nor the author can accept responsibility for any errors or omissions, however caused. Nor can any responsibility be accepted for loss or damage as a result of reading this publication.

Published by Novaro Publishing Ltd, 2 Speedwell Drive, Lindfield, West Sussex
e: publish@novaropublishing.com.

Copyright © Alex Tofalides, 2025
The moral right of the author has been asserted.

All rights reserved. Apart from any fair dealing for the purposes of research or private study, criticism or review, this publication may only be reproduced, stored or transmitted in any form or by any means with the prior permission in writing of the publisher.

ISBN: 978-1-0685644-2-0

A CIP catalogue record for this book is available from the British Library.

Designed by Chantel Barnett, Clear Design CC Ltd

For further details about our titles and our authors, see:
www.novaropublishing.com

Cover photographs with the permission of Constantinos Kyprianou, Light Memories.

FIGHTING FOR YOUR DREAM

MASTERING RESILIENCE AND PERFORMING WHEN IT REALLY MATTERS

ALEX TOFALIDES

To my family and to all those chasing a dream – never give up

CONTENTS

Foreword   1
Theo Paphitis

Introduction   5

Part 1

1. Dream it, believe it, achieve it   15
2. Mastering the mind   20
3. When it goes against you   25
4. Choose your battle   30
5. Upsets and underdogs   36
6. Team dynamics   43
7. Fighting back   49

Part 2

8. Taking responsibility   61
9. Mental preparation   71
10. Process and routine   79
11. Psychologically aware   85
12. Data analysis   93
13. Training and sparring   98
14. Negative thoughts   104
15. Narrative building   111
16. Competing with the best   116

17.	Holistic effort	124
18.	Luxembourg	129

Conclusion: Paris 2024 — 147

Appendices

1. Alex's fencing career — 167
2. Terms in fencing — 170
3. Terms in performance pyschology — 175
4. World-class mental skills in fencing — 179

Acknowledgements — 187

FOREWORD

When I first heard about Alex Tofalides's dream, I was struck by two things: its sheer scale and the fierce determination behind it. In a world that is often all about quick wins and instant gratification, setting out at seven years old to become an Olympic fencer and then pursuing that goal for more than two decades borders on the heroic. As someone who left Cyprus as a child and went on to build businesses against the odds, I know what it means to chase a dream that others find impractical or even impossible. That is why I was honoured when Alex asked me to contribute a foreword to his book. I met Alex's family through business in a partnership that led to friendship, as good business often can.

Fighting for Your Dream is not just a sports memoir. It is a blueprint for anyone who aspires to achieve something extraordinary, whether in sport, business or life. Over the course of these pages, Alex invites us into the mind of an underdog who refused to accept the status quo – and who doesn't love an underdog? We witness him navigating the political complexities of elite sport, rebuilding after injury, funding cuts and heartbreak, and even coping with the devastating loss of his father, all while remaining focused on a singular goal. Each setback becomes a lesson; each disappointment, an opportunity to refine his strategy.

What emerges from this story is a set of principles that are as relevant in the boardroom as they are on the piste. Alex writes honestly about the importance of mental mastery under pressure and explains how thought patterns shape outcomes and why self-awareness is fundamental to success. He demonstrates that taking full responsibility for your destiny, rather than relying on external structures, is both liberating and demanding. He shows how to deconstruct failure, build systems and habits that endure, and craft a narrative that sustains you when others doubt you. As an entrepreneur, I recognise these principles intimately: the ability to adapt; to analyse data and make decisions under stress; to invest in the small processes that lead to big results.

This book also reminds us that dreams need oxygen. Alex's journey underscores the value of a strong support network of mentors and team-mates, who challenge and uplift you, and of the communities that shape your identity. In choosing to represent Cyprus, he embraced his heritage and honoured his father's legacy. In stepping into the role of athlete, coach and tactician all at once, he learned the power of self-coaching and strategic thinking. His story proves that success is seldom the result of talent alone; it is born from resilience, reflection and relentless preparation.

One of the qualities I most admire in *Fighting for Your Dream* is its honesty. Alex does not shy away from the dark moments: the nights of self-doubt, the fear of not being good enough, the pressure of finances and politics. Instead, he uses them to illustrate how negative thoughts

FOREWORD

can sabotage even the strongest performers and offers practical techniques for emotional regulation and reframing setbacks. He writes openly about the anger he felt when a bout slipped away and about the quiet joy of seeing his mother's tears when he finally qualified for Paris 2024. These candid reflections make his eventual triumph not just a sporting achievement but a testament to the strength of the human spirit.

As you read this book, you will find yourself on the edge of your seat during the final qualification match in Luxembourg. You will learn what it means to train with Olympic champions and how to break down an opponent's style with forensic precision and strategy. More importantly, you will come away with insights you can apply to your own ambitions, whether you are leading a company, starting a side hustle or balancing family and career. Like Alex, you will realise that the Olympic moment does not mark an end point; it reveals who you have become through the fight.

I am proud to see a fellow Cypriot make history on the world stage, and I am equally proud to see him share his journey with such generosity and depth. Alex's story is proof that dreams are worth pursuing, no matter how long they take or how many obstacles lie in the way. I hope his words inspire you, as they have inspired me, to think strategically, to believe fiercely and, above all, to never give up.

Theo Paphitis
Retail magnate and former Dragons' Den panellist
Rymans | Boux Avenue | Robert Dyas | London Graphic Centre

can sabotage even the strongest performers and offers practical techniques for emotional regulation and reframing setbacks. He writes openly about the anger he felt when a bout slipped away and about the quiet joy of seeing his mother's tears when he finally qualified for Paris 2024. These candid reflections make his eventual triumph not just a sporting achievement but a testament to the strength of the human spirit.

As you read this book, you will find yourself on the edge of your seat during the final qualification match in Luxembourg. You will learn what it means to train with Olympic champions and how to break down an opponent's style with forensic precision and strategy. More importantly, you will come away with insights you can apply to your own ambitions, whether you are leading a company, starting a side hustle or balancing family and career. Like Alex, you will realise that the Olympic moment does not mark an end point; it reveals who you have become through the fight.

I am proud to see a fellow Cypriot make history on the world stage, and I am equally proud to see him share his journey with such generosity and depth. Alex's story is proof that dreams are worth pursuing, no matter how long they take or how many obstacles lie in the way. I hope his words inspire you, as they have inspired me, to think strategically, to believe fiercely and, above all, to never give up.

Theo Paphitis
Retail magnate and former Dragons' Den panellist
Rymans | Boux Avenue | Robert Dyas | London Graphic Centre

INTRODUCTION

On 26 April 2024, I stood on the fencing piste in Luxembourg, ready for the most significant match of my life: the final of the European Olympic Qualifier. One day. One match. One ticket to the Olympic Games. The culmination of over 20 years of dedication, sacrifice and relentless training had come down to this singular moment.

After narrowly missing qualification for the London, Rio and Tokyo Olympics, it felt like my final chance to realise the dream I had chased since childhood. For three years, I had visualised this day with cinematic precision: the final point scored, the moment I removed my mask, looked up to the sky and imagined my father smiling down from above, shook my opponent's hand and turned to embrace my mother with the words, 'we did it'.

This was no ordinary competition. It was a winner-takes-all event, where 30 of Europe's finest fencers were battling for a single, coveted spot at the Games. Everyone who stepped into that hall knew they were fighting for the biggest prize fencing had to offer. In a tournament of this magnitude, it wasn't just about skill, it was about who could hold their nerve when everything was on the line.

I had been here before. Three years earlier in Madrid, I stood in the same position, so close, only to fall short. The heartbreak of that day became fuel for the years that followed. And this time, I was determined to leave absolutely nothing to chance.

As I donned my mask and stepped onto the piste, I knew that regardless of the result, I had done everything in my power to be ready, physically, technically and psychologically. I had planned for this moment backwards from the final point, dedicating every ounce of energy to ensure that when it mattered most, I was in control.

For three years, I had lived this match in my mind. I'd seen the final touch, heard the roar of the crowd, felt the embrace with my mum. I'd seen it so many times, it didn't feel like a dream anymore, it felt inevitable.

Over the previous seven years, since switching from representing Great Britain to Cyprus, I had become more than just an athlete. I had become my own coach, psychologist and tactician. I studied every potential opponent, learned their patterns, identified their weaknesses and honed my strategy so I could make them play my game. I had done my 10,000 hours and I knew what it would take to win.

This book is not just about one match or one victory. It's about the entire journey, the failures, the breakthroughs, the quiet moments of doubt and the fire that kept me going. It's about what it takes to chase an Olympic dream, and, more importantly, what it takes to keep chasing when everything seems to be against you.

Throughout these pages, you'll find pivotal moments from my life and career, interwoven with powerful lessons drawn from psychology, elite sport and high-performance living. Whether you're an athlete, entrepreneur, student or simply someone striving for more, this book

INTRODUCTION

is a guide to building the resilience, focus and mindset needed to perform under pressure.

This is the story of how I became Cyprus's first-ever Olympic fencer. And it's an invitation for you to build the tools, frameworks and inner strength to fight the battles on your terrain.

I have come to believe that there are several key principles that underpin success and throughout this book you will see how these principles played out in my journey. These principles include the power of belief and dreams, the importance of determination, the ability to adapt to changing circumstances and the value of a strong support network. Beyond these, I also learned the significance of developing solid processes, mastering the art of compartmentalisation and, perhaps most importantly, gaining a deep understanding of yourself.

The power of belief and dreams

At the heart of every journey is a dream whose power cannot be overstated. From the age of seven, when I first picked up a fencing sword, I dreamed of one day competing at the Olympics. That dream, often intangible and far off, served as my guiding star for more than two decades. It pushed me to wake up every day and train, even when it seemed like progress was slow or non-existent. It gave me the resilience to come back stronger after every failure and it provided me with the focus needed to block out distractions and setbacks along the way.

Belief, however, is not just about dreaming big. It is about having the unwavering conviction that, with enough effort and dedication, those dreams can become a reality. The world is full of people with talent, but talent alone is rarely enough. What separates those who succeed from those who fall short is often the belief that they can and will achieve what they set out to do. This kind of belief doesn't come from outside validation; it comes from within, and it requires a deep understanding of yourself and your abilities. I didn't always have this belief, especially in the early days of my career. But as the years went on, as I fought through countless competitions and training sessions, I developed an inner confidence that became the cornerstone of my success.

Determination: the relentless pursuit of a goal

If belief is the fuel that drives you, then determination is the engine that keeps you going when the road gets tough. There were many times throughout my career when I questioned whether the dream of reaching the Olympics was worth the sacrifices. After missing out on qualification for the London, Rio, and Tokyo Olympics, it would have been easy to give up. Injuries, lack of funding and the mental strain of constant failure could have derailed me. But what kept me moving forward was an unwavering determination, a refusal to quit, no matter how many times I was knocked down.

Determination is about more than just grit; it is about resilience. It is the ability to take the hits that life throws at you and to get back up, each time with renewed focus and drive. In the world of fencing, as in life, the key is not how many times you get hit, but how quickly you can recover and learn from those setbacks. Every loss, every failure and every disappointment became a stepping stone on the path to success. It was through those moments of struggle that I learned the most about myself and what I was capable of.

INTRODUCTION

Adapting to challenges

No journey is linear and my road to the Olympics was no exception. Along the way, I faced countless obstacles that required me to adapt my approach. Whether it was dealing with physical injuries, adjusting to the changing dynamics of the fencing world or finding new ways to balance my personal and professional life with my athletic career, adaptation was a constant theme.

One of the biggest lessons I learned was that the ability to adapt is what separates those who succeed from those who fall short. In fencing, matches can change in an instant and the fencer who can read their opponent, adjust their tactics and make split-second decisions is the one who will come out on top. The same is true in life. Whether it's changing your strategy in business, pivoting when your plans fall apart or adjusting to unexpected challenges, the ability to stay flexible and adapt is crucial to long-term success.

A support network to keep you going

No one achieves success alone and I am no exception. Throughout my journey, I was fortunate to have an incredible support network in my coach, my family, my friends and my team-mates, who believed in me even when I doubted myself. Their encouragement, advice and sometimes tough love were instrumental in keeping me on track, especially during the hardest moments.

Behind every great athlete is a team of people who provide the foundation for success. My coaches were with me every step of the way, helping me fine-tune my technique, develop strategies and push beyond my limits. My family, especially my mother, was there from the start, signing me up for that first fencing class when I was seven and supporting me through every high and low. And my friends and teammates provided the camaraderie and encouragement that kept me going through the toughest training sessions and most difficult competitions.

Processes: the path to mastery

Success is not achieved through one-off moments of brilliance, but through the meticulous perfection of daily habits and processes. Throughout my career, I developed a set of processes that allowed me to perform at my best, whether it was during training, competition or recovery. These processes became second nature, preparing with my mental warm-up, structuring my physical training for peak performance and developing tactics tailored to each opponent.

Mastery comes from consistently honing these processes, learning from every experience and refining your approach over time. Whether in sport or in life, those who succeed are the ones who dedicate themselves to improving, day by day, no matter how small the gains may seem in the moment.

Compartmentalisation: the art of focus

One of the most important skills I developed during my career was compartmentalisation: the ability to separate different parts of my life and focus fully on the task at hand. When I was training, my mind was 100 percent on fencing. When I was working on my business, I was fully focused on that. This skill was essential in helping me manage the various demands of my life, from training and competition to my personal relationships and professional career.

Compartmentalisation is not about ignoring the other parts of your life; it's about giving your full attention to what is in front of you at any given moment. It's about being present, fully engaged and not allowing distractions or worries to pull you away from your goals.

Understanding yourself

Ultimately, the most important lesson I've learned is that success, whether in sport, business or life, comes from understanding yourself. You must take full responsibility for your actions, decisions and outcomes. You must learn what works for you, what doesn't and be willing to continuously evolve. The journey to the Olympics was not just about becoming a better fencer; it was about becoming a better person. It was about developing the self-awareness to know my strengths and weaknesses, the discipline to refine my processes and the resilience to keep moving forward, no matter what.

As you read this book, you will see how these lessons played out for me. Whether you are an athlete, a professional or someone chasing a personal goal, my hope is that this story will inspire you to push beyond your limits, to never give up on your dreams and to believe that, with enough determination, adaptability and self-belief, anything is possible.

PART 1

1

DREAM IT, BELIEVE IT, ACHIEVE IT

When I first picked up a fencing sword at the age of seven, the sport felt like a game. You put on your kit, you faced your opponent, and you gave everything you had. Win or lose, you shook hands and walked away smiling. There were no outside pressures, no rankings to consider, no career-defining moments, just the thrill of competing and the joy of improving.

Those early days were some of the most carefree moments of my fencing career. When I struggled with doubt or setbacks later in life, I often found myself mentally drifting back to that time, when I fenced for the love of it, with a smile on my face. Rose tinted or not, those memories kept me going when things felt tough.

When I was 14, I attended a fencing camp in Poland. By that point, I'd built a reputation as someone who fought hard but lacked true talent. I was always good, but never quite good enough to win. My nemesis, Tom Allen, was a constant reminder of that. Every time I faced him, I'd lose and not just narrowly. These were one-sided encounters: 10–1, 10–2, even 10–0. Facing Tom made me question whether I really had what it took. No matter how hard I tried, I couldn't seem to break through.

The Polish camp changed that. The environment was intense. Fencers trained with relentless energy, pushing the boundaries of technique and mental endurance. For three weeks, I struggled to keep pace, but I kept showing up, absorbing everything I could. When I returned home, something had shifted.

I faced Tom again shortly after. This time, I narrowly lost 3-2. I hadn't beaten him yet, but it was the first time I felt that I could. That moment lit a fire in me. I realised that talent wasn't everything. Belief and preparation could bridge the gap. This was the start of something deeper: my belief that if I worked hard enough and prepared well enough, I could achieve anything.

In 2010, I qualified to represent Great Britain at the inaugural Youth Olympics in Singapore. Being at a multi-sport event and seeing all the other athletes, of course, motivated me to train harder to compete in the Olympics. However, one specific aspect would motivate me more than I could have imagined and still does to this day. On each of our rooms, the Team GB staff had put a poster with a different quote. On my shared dorm, the banner read: 'Dream it, believe it, achieve it'.

That phrase became my mantra. Every day from that moment forward, I reminded myself: if I could hold on to that belief, no setback would be insurmountable. If I could dream it and believe it, I could achieve it.

The role of environment

Looking back, I now realise that my environment played a pivotal role in my development as an athlete. In *Bounce*, a book about the true nature of talent, Matthew Syed finds that while it takes hard work to realise it, outcomes are often driven by circumstance. He highlights how proximity to top-level facilities, coaching and opportunities can dramatically influence outcomes. For me, my circumstances were incredibly fortunate.

By the time I was 13, I had joined Salle Paul at William Ellis School in Highgate, just a ten-minute walk from home. It's impossible to overstate how fortunate I was. Training in one of Britain's top fencing clubs wasn't just about learning skills; it meant regular exposure to elite-level coaching and constant sparring with some of the best fencers in the country. My coaches, Ziemek Wojcieowski and Maciej Wojtowiak, both worked with the British national team. Without that level of guidance, my career might have been very different.

Matthew Syed describes this as the golden-opportunity effect. He explains that elite performers often emerge from environments that provide both access and inspiration, whether it's musicians living near elite tutors or tech innovators with access to key networks. For me, having a world-class training facility within walking distance provided the opportunity to develop my fencing skills in an environment where excellence was the norm.

Of course, talent still plays a role, but opportunity opens the door. My success was built on both.

Dreams and visualisation

While environment played a key role in my development, belief became my greatest weapon and visualisation was crucial to building it.

Michael Phelps, the most decorated Olympian of all time, was known for his incredible use of mental rehearsal. Phelps visualised his races in meticulous detail: the sound of the crowd, the feel of the water, every stroke, every breath. By the time Phelps competed, he had already won that race hundreds of times in his mind.

I used the same strategy before major competitions. Before my Olympic qualifier in Luxembourg in 2024, I spent months visualising success. Every morning, I would sit quietly and imagine myself fencing in that final. I pictured stepping onto the piste, seeing my opponent's actions, adjusting my tactics and ultimately scoring the final point. By rehearsing it repeatedly, my mind accepted that scenario as achievable.

My former coach, Ziemek, once told me a powerful story about Fabio Dal Zotto, the Italian fencer who won Olympic gold in 1976. In the lead-up to the Games, Dal Zotto would wake up every morning, stand on an imaginary podium and sing the Italian national anthem to himself as if he had already won. That constant mental rehearsal didn't just strengthen his belief, it conditioned his mind to expect success.

The day before the Olympic qualifier, I stood in my room and did the same thing. I imagined standing on the podium, hearing the Cypriot national anthem play. I visualised it so many times that, when the moment finally arrived, it felt familiar like I had been there before.

This kind of visualisation and belief was crucial for one of Britain's greatest athletes, Andy Murray. For years, Murray fought to establish himself at the top level of tennis. He was consistently overshadowed by Roger Federer, Rafa Nadal and Novak Djokovic, three of the greatest players in history. Despite his immense talent, Murray couldn't quite break through in the biggest moments.

That changed at the 2012 Olympics in London. Weeks earlier, Murray had lost to Federer in the Wimbledon final and the pressure was immense. But in the Olympic final, Murray played with a new sense of belief. He dominated Federer, winning in straight sets to secure

Olympic gold. That victory, in front of a home crowd, gave him the confidence he had been searching for. Just weeks later, he won his first grand-slam event at the US Open.

Murray's success wasn't just about improved technique, it was about belief. He had seen himself winning in his mind. Once he experienced that breakthrough, his mindset shifted. He knew he belonged at the very top.

The road to the Olympics is rarely straightforward. I didn't qualify for the Games on my first, second or even third attempt. But that dream never left me. The belief I had built through visualisation and preparation allowed me to keep going. When I finally qualified for Paris 2024, it was the result of years spent building belief, one point, one training session and one mental rehearsal at a time.

Dream it. Believe it. Achieve it.

2

MASTERING THE MIND

There's a moment in every athlete's career when self-belief becomes the deciding factor. The mental shift from doubt to conviction can transform performance. For me, one of the biggest turning points in my career came at the Modling World Cup.

It was the final world cup of the season, held in Austria, and it was my last chance to qualify for the British team at the Under-20 World Championships. It wasn't just another competition; it was a make-or-break moment that would determine if I would qualify for the biggest junior event in the fencing calendar. For months, I had known this was my last opportunity to book a place on the team.

In the lead-up to this, the squad was extremely competitive. I was battling to secure one of the top three spots for the World Championships. Husayn Rosowsky and Jamie Fitzgerald were performing strongly, leaving just one place up for grabs, which had come down to James Davis and me.

James wasn't just another rival; he was someone I had trained with since I was 13. A tall, fast and technically gifted fencer, James would later go on to become a European champion and a two-time Olympian. We were part of the same training group, constantly pushing each other to improve. For years, we had been team-mates, yet here we were, two friends fighting for a single place on the British team.

Going into the competition, I needed to finish two rounds ahead of James to qualify for the individual event. The pressure was suffocating and I barely slept the night before, perhaps one or two hours at most. But that morning, I made a conscious decision: instead of obsessing over James's results, I would focus entirely on my own performance. I couldn't control what James did, but I could control my own actions.

I won five matches and lost one, leaving me ranked 40th for the knock-out stages. In my first elimination bout, I defeated an Israeli fencer. Next came Maciej Wlosek, the under-20 European vice champion: a tough opponent and someone I wasn't expected to beat. Somehow, I found a way, winning 15–12.

Moments later, I heard the roar of James Davis celebrating a victory. That roar reminded me that my task wasn't over. I knew I needed to keep winning; now I'd have to win two more matches and get a medal, something I hadn't done before.

In my round-of-16 match, I faced Robert Gatai of Hungary, ranked in the world's top five at the time. I managed to win, narrowly advancing to the quarter-finals. Next up was Race Imboden, a future world number one and Olympic medallist. Against the odds, I beat him 15–8, marking my first-ever world medal at the U20 level.

Unfortunately, James Davis had also reached the semi-finals, which meant that, unless I won the tournament outright, I wouldn't qualify. My semi-final opponent was Moritz Kroplin, the reigning U20

European champion. A tall, powerful and physical German fencer, the match became a war of attrition. I edged the victory 15–13.

The final was now a winner-takes-all showdown between me and James Davis. We had trained together for years; we knew each other's strengths and weaknesses. The match became a tense, back-and-forth battle, leaving us tied at 14–14, one touch away from qualification.

That final point felt like a coin toss, fate deciding my future. But somehow, I found the right action. I attacked, my light came on and I had won 15–14. For the first time ever, two British fencers had finished first and second at a world cup. Incredibly, both James and I had qualified for the World Championships, something that had only been possible if we had both finished in the top two.

That day, I learned three powerful lessons:

- Sleep doesn't affect short-term performance as much as we imagine.
- The power of focusing on one point at a time.
- Nothing is impossible if you maintain belief and determination.

Those moments of clarity would shape my mindset for years to come.

Learning to manage the mind

The mental discipline I applied at Modling drew heavily on techniques described in *The Chimp Paradox* by Dr Steve Peters (Vermilion, 2011), a psychiatrist who help to transform the performance of elite British cyclists, such as Chris Hoy, Bradley Wiggins and Victoria Pendleton. Dr Peters breaks the brain into three key parts:

- **The chimp**: fast, instinctive and emotional. The impulsive voice that reacts under pressure.

- **The human**: calm, rational and logical. This side controls strategy, composure and focus.

- **The computer**: a bank of stored habits and experiences that dictate automatic responses. The computer is 20 times faster than the human and four times faster than the chimp, which is why pre-programmed mental skills can outperform rational thinking in the heat of competition.

The Modling World Cup experience allowed me to programme my computer with three vital autopilots that would stay with me throughout my career:

- Focus on one point at a time: the ability to mentally reset after each point, regardless of the score or situation.

- Believe that nothing is impossible: the deep conviction that no deficit, no opponent and no situation was beyond my ability to overcome.

- Understand that sleep doesn't always impact immediate performance: I hadn't trained for this before, but the Modling experience taught me that even on minimal rest, I could still perform if my mindset was right.

For Peters, the key to mastering pressure is programming your computer so thoroughly that you instinctively know what to do in high-stress moments. The conscious mind can only process so much information, but when the computer is trained correctly, you can perform without hesitation.

Sleep and performance

Despite getting just two hours of sleep the night before the final, I defied conventional wisdom and performed at my absolute best. A famous sporting example comes from Michael Jordan's iconic performance in game 5 of the 1997 NBA Finals, known as the 'flu game'.

Michael Jordan is widely considered the greatest basketball player of all time, a six-time NBA champion and a five-time NBA Most Valuable Player. The NBA finals are the championship series of the National Basketball Association, the highest level of professional basketball in the world.

In this game, Jordan had been battling severe illness, reportedly suffering from food poisoning. Despite feeling physically drained, he scored 38 points, leading the Chicago Bulls to a crucial victory. Jordan's performance proved that mental strength, preparation and belief can carry you through even when the body is under immense strain.

At Modling, my body had been trained to operate under pressure and, because I trusted my process, my mind took control and guided me through the day. That experience gave me confidence later in my career. On nights when anxiety or insomnia threatened to derail my preparation, I reminded myself that I could still perform at a high level, even with minimal rest.

3

WHEN IT GOES AGAINST YOU

The year was 2011 and I was 18. London was hosting the following year's Olympics. For British athletes, this presented a once-in-a-lifetime opportunity: a chance to compete at a home Games with extra places for the home nation available. I knew my odds were slim, but there was still a chance. I had worked relentlessly, reached seventh in the under-20 world rankings and believed I could break into the four-man squad that would represent Great Britain at the Games. Despite some personal best results at senior level, I was unable to make the four man team finishing the season ranked eighth. This Olympic games had unfortunately come too early in my career.

Jessica Ennis and the power of resilience

During that period, I found inspiration in the story of Jessica Ennis, one of Britain's most celebrated Olympic champions. In the lead-up to the 2008 Beijing Olympics, Ennis suffered a career-threatening stress fracture in her right foot. Unable to compete at the Games, she watched from the sidelines as her competitors excelled on the world's biggest stage.

But rather than allowing that setback to define her, Ennis used it as motivation. Over the next four years, she transformed herself physically and mentally. By the time London 2012 arrived, she had improved in nearly every event within the heptathlon.

She dominated the competition and became Olympic champion on home soil. Jessica's story reinforced something I was learning first-hand: setbacks are inevitable, but it's how you respond that defines you.

Changing of the guard: the politics of sport

That period marked a turning point in British fencing. The arrival of a new performance director coincided with increased competition for Olympic places and suddenly the politics within the sport intensified. Coaches manoeuvred to position their students in the best possible light and alliances began to form.

One of them was my personal coach, Maciej Wojtowiak. Dedicated and supportive, his focus shifted when he accepted the role of coach to the women's foil team. Since I was on the men's foil team, it created a logistical challenge. He was now spending long periods away in training camps with the women. I assumed that since Ziemek Wojcieowski was still coaching the men's foil team, I could arrange lessons with him while Maciej was away.

I remember visiting Maciej at his house to discuss this. When I asked if I could also take lessons with Ziemek, his response was casual: 'sure, I don't care'. As an 18-year-old, I didn't pick up on the underlying tension. I believed everything was fine and continued training with both coaches as the Olympic selection race heated up.

After the Olympics, Maciej set his sights on securing the men's foil coaching position. Working closely with the performance director, he succeeded in having Ziemek removed from his role. Maciej was temporarily installed as head coach.

The world-class performance programme

In September 2013, British Fencing held a selection day to determine which athletes would be inducted onto the world-class performance programme, a crucial pathway for elite fencers. Although I was already part of the programme, I still needed to demonstrate my value in this fresh round of assessments. Despite being ranked in the top ten in the world at U20 level at the time, I discovered I hadn't been selected.

A week later, I was informed that I would be given a three-month probation period. During this time, I would need to take a lesson with Maciej every day and any sign of negative behaviour would result in my immediate removal. For three months, I bit my tongue and got on with my training. I swallowed my pride, ignored provocations and stayed focused. Ultimately, I was reinstated on the programme. Fortunately, a highly respected, new coach, Andrei Klushin, arrived, which provided a fresh start.

Choosing your battles wisely

That experience taught me a valuable lessons: the importance of choosing your battles. At the time, my natural instinct was to fight back against what I believed was unfair treatment. In meetings with the performance director, I became fixated on proving them wrong. I was so focused on defending my position that I lost sight of what truly mattered: securing my place and moving forward.

I vividly remember one heated meeting where my dad accompanied me. On the car ride home, he gave me advice that has stayed with me ever since: 'you've got to decide what's more important, proving you're right or getting what you want'.

I realised I had wasted valuable energy trying to win arguments rather than focusing on what I needed to do to succeed. From that point forward, I learned that sometimes the smartest move is to stay quiet, swallow your pride and play the long game.

Injuries: managing the physical toll

In the aftermath of my struggles with selection, my body began to break down. Years of intense training had pushed me to my limits and I was battling persistent injuries.

The most challenging of these was patellar tendinopathy, a painful inflammation in the knee tendon. I still remember the 2011/12 season when it first flared up. My training load went from six to seven matches a day to just one or two, sometimes none if the pain was unbearable.

One day, our Team GB physiotherapist, Ed Mias, pulled me aside. Pointing across the room at my teammate, Jamie Kenber, he said: 'that's your future if you don't manage your injury properly'.

Jamie was one of the most talented fencers in the squad but had been plagued by injuries. Ed's warning was blunt but necessary. He told me that I had a choice: take responsibility for managing my injury now or risk losing everything I'd worked for.

That conversation forced me to adopt a new approach. I committed to a holistic strategy with strengthening exercises, mobility work and strict recovery routines. I learnt that injuries weren't just physical battles; they required mental discipline as well.

Desirable difficulty

In his book *Bounce*, Matthew Syed talks about the critical role of setbacks in elite performance. He explores the concept of desirable difficulty: the idea that obstacles and adversity can actually improve performance when approached correctly.

In fencing, this idea rang especially true. Learning to adapt my training around my injury forced me to become smarter, more efficient and more self-reliant. It also taught me patience, the kind that only comes from understanding that growth isn't always linear.

Looking back, I now understand that some of my biggest leaps forward came after my hardest setbacks.

The power of letting go

If there's one final lesson I took from that period, it was that sometimes you have to let go of what you can't control to focus on what you can. Whether it was the politics of selection, the frustration of injury or the bitterness of feeling wronged, I realised that holding onto those things would only drag me down.

Success in sport, and in life, often comes down to resilience: the ability to absorb setbacks, refocus and keep moving forward. If I could go back and face those struggles again, I would do one thing differently: I would forgive sooner, not for anyone else's sake, but for my own.

4

CHOOSE YOUR BATTLE

One of the key lessons I learned as I progressed in my fencing career was to always look for glitches in the system, whether in my own fencing style or in others'. Identifying and exploiting these weaknesses can provide a crucial advantage. This concept isn't limited to fencing; it applies to any competitive environment. In sports like tennis or football, underdogs often win when they spot and capitalise on flaws in a stronger opponent's game.

A classic example came at the European Football Championship in 2004, when Greece, a complete outsider, defied all expectations to win the tournament. Under coach Otto Rehhagel, the Greek team identified the glitches in more technically skilled teams like France and Portugal. Rather than outplaying them with flair, they applied a disciplined, structured game built around defence and set pieces. They made giants crumble by playing the game on their terms.

Like Netflix, which saw a flaw in Blockbuster's late-fee model and capitalised by offering online rentals without overdue penalties. Eventually, they revolutionised the film industry, while Blockbuster disappeared.

For me, recognising tactical inefficiencies and system flaws became a key way to punch above my weight. I was never going to be the biggest or the fastest. But I could be the most prepared. That mindset shaped everything that followed.

Moving to senior level: adapting or falling away

After my time at under-20 level, where I won a U20 world cup, earned three European medals and achieved a top ten ranking in the world, I faced the next great challenge: transitioning to senior-level fencing.

This moment, going from a big fish in a small pond to a small fish in a vast one, is where many promising athletes fall away. In U17 and U20 fencing, you can succeed with a narrower skill set. You're competing against similarly aged and physically matched peers. But in senior fencing, you face athletes aged 20 to 40, who are stronger, more experienced and vastly more technically complete.

I'd been getting by with two signature moves, one attack and one counter. But that wasn't going to cut it anymore. You're found out quickly at senior level if you don't evolve.

One of our performance analysts pulled me aside and said, 'Toff, I've reviewed your matches. You can be world class, but you need to broaden your game'.

The suggestion? Add a parry riposte to my defensive arsenal. Until then, I relied heavily on counterattacks. But with a proper parry riposte, an action that meets the opponent's blade, you add unpredictability. The attacker doesn't know if you'll parry or counter and that creates hesitation.

Implementing new tactics

Here's how I approached technical and tactical changes, a process I still use today:

- Identify the new move.
- Practise it in private lessons for one to two weeks.
- Test it on lower-level opponents for another two weeks.
- Introduce it gradually into training bouts with better opponents.
- Use it in real competitions.

It's a six-to-eight-week process that assumes total commitment. Major changes like these are best tackled in pre-season. During the competitive season, it's risky.

Short-term pain, long-term gain

In October 2013, pre-season, I committed to making this change. Instantly, my training-win rate dropped from 80 percent to 20–30 percent. I was losing constantly. My ego was in pieces. My teammates assumed I had declined and, to be fair, it looked that way. But I stuck with it. I reminded myself: short-term pain, long-term gain.

Two months later, I began scoring regularly with the new actions. That slow climb was one of the most satisfying experiences in my career. Not because I was winning again, but because I had broken through a psychological barrier: accepting that losing temporarily could lead to long-term progress.

The golden minute

That improvement came just in time. I entered the British Senior Championships with something to prove. It wasn't just about results. I needed to show that I had evolved. That I could win at the senior level. In the final, I faced Marcus Mepstead, who was older, more experienced and ranked higher. Our styles clashed: he was ultra-defensive; I was aggressive and instinctive. I knew I needed to take him somewhere unfamiliar. That's where the golden minute came in.

Fencing has a rule: if the score is tied after three periods, there's a final one-minute bout. Priority is randomly assigned to one fencer. If neither scores, the one with priority wins.

But the rules had a loophole. If a minute passes in each period without action, the match jumps ahead to the next one. After three such periods, it jumps to the golden minute early.

I had tried this before — and failed. Once against Maxime Pauty, a future Olympic champion, I used the tactic and got priority. But he scored with four seconds left. Another time, a teammate hit me with one second to go.

Still, I believed in the tactic. It was bold, different and it gave me control. So, I played the long game. I defended, refused to attack, forced passive calls and took the match into the golden minute.

Choose your own terrain

My decision wasn't random. It was rooted in philosophy, specifically the teachings of Sun Tzu. He was, a Chinese military general and strategist from the 5th century BC, who wrote *The Art of War*, a timeless treatise on warfare still studied in leadership, military and business circles. One of his most powerful principles is: 'he who knows when he can fight and when he cannot will be victorious'.

It isn't just about war; it's about life, business and sport. The idea is simple: don't fight battles on your opponent's terms. Change the terrain. Shift the conditions. Make them uncomfortable.

That's what the golden minute did. Marcus was used to controlling the rhythm. Suddenly, he had to adapt. And when the time came, he blinked first.

He attacked with 17 seconds left. I was ready. I scored. Then again and again. I won the title 4–1.

Programme yourself mentally

It wasn't just a tactical victory. It was mental. I didn't react emotionally under pressure, like Steve Peters's chimp, or rely on being on a rational human. Instead, I had programmed myself with routines and processes that took over when it really mattered. That day my computer was running as perfectly as Steve Peters could wish.

During the golden minute, my emotional chimp instinct when I was under pressure would have been to attack Marcus most likely resulting in losing the match. Instead months of programming my computer with my new defensive skills enabled me to execute my tactics in the way I had trained and win the match. That day, my computer was running perfectly. I resisted the urge to chase. I stuck to the plan. The victory came not just from fencing skill, but from managing pressure.

Transforming for real, not overnight

This chapter of my career taught me that transformation doesn't happen with declarations. It happens in the daily grind. Losing in training. Changing habits. Controlling nerves. Learning from philosophy and psychology. Spotting glitches. Rewiring instinct. Backing yourself. That's what it means to transform. And it set the tone for everything that came after.

5

UPSETS AND UNDERDOGS

In every competitive arena, from sports to business, the underdog occupies a unique position. Seemingly weaker and less skilled, the underdog enjoys reduced expectations and psychological freedom. Often, these offer a crucial advantage, as pressure weighs heavily on their opponents, who carry the burden of expectation. To triumph, the underdog must carefully create a plan, playing to their strengths, reshaping the terms of engagement and forcing the favourite out of their comfort zone.

Shift your focus

Before a crucial match or event, it's natural to feel nerves and anxiety. Athletes often become absorbed by internal pressures: the importance of the outcome, personal fears or self-doubt. Yet one of the most powerful mental shifts involves stepping away from these internal preoccupations and directing your attention towards your opponent's state of mind.

We often forget that opponents, even those who seem invincible, carry their own vulnerabilities and burdens. Shifting your focus externally and considering what your opponent might be experiencing can profoundly alter your psychological approach. Perhaps your opponent feels immense expectation due to past successes; maybe they're managing an injury, fatigue or personal distractions. Recognising these factors helps humanise them, reduces the sense of intimidation and provides tangible psychological leverage. This external focus can free you from anxiety and sharpen your strategic clarity, turning the opponent's strengths into vulnerabilities.

Craft the plan: Pep Guardiola v Jose Mourinho

Every athlete has a distinct approach, a personal philosophy that defines their tactics and style. Broadly speaking, athletes fall into two camps: those who seek perfection through beauty and style; and those whose singular focus is effectiveness and victory, regardless of aesthetics.

In football, two iconic figures embody this divide: Pep Guardiola and Jose Mourinho. Guardiola, renowned for his elegant and attack-oriented football, sees sport as an art form. He believes winning with style is as important as victory itself. Mourinho, however, embodies pragmatism: victory at any cost, effectiveness above all. He is willing to sacrifice aesthetics to exploit an opponent's weaknesses, disrupting their rhythm and turning their strengths into vulnerabilities.

Their legendary battles provide invaluable lessons. In the 2010 Champions League semi-final, Guardiola's Barcelona, widely considered the best football team in history, faced Mourinho's Inter Milan. Barcelona, with their flowing, beautiful style, were overwhelming favourites. Mourinho meticulously constructed a plan that neutralised Barcelona's rhythm. He deliberately conceded possession, allowed Barcelona to overextend themselves and struck ruthlessly on the counterattack. Guardiola's side, accustomed to dictating the game, became increasingly frustrated. Their composure frayed, their attacks became rushed and their confidence waned. Mourinho's Inter triumphed against expectations, not because of superior talent, but through disciplined execution of a carefully crafted tactical and psychological plan.

La Coruña World Cup 2014

At the La Coruña World Cup in Spain in 2014, I faced Peter Joppich, one of foil fencing's greats, a four-time individual world champion. Simply reaching this round was significant; facing such an elite opponent was daunting. However, I always believed that with the right preparation, any opponent could be defeated by pairing your strengths against their weaknesses.

Our analyst, Dai Fulcher, had provided extensive breakdowns of Joppich's style: his favoured attacks, preferred defences and, crucially, the areas of the piste where he scored most frequently. This allowed me to craft a clear strategy: fence defensively, control distance and patiently exploit his predictable habits.

Several factors favoured me: the early 9am match time meant Joppich competed without recent bouts. Possibly underestimating me as an unknown young fencer also created openings for surprise.

The match unfolded precisely as planned. Joppich became frustrated, predictable and I secured a stunning 15–10 victory. This instilled genuine belief in my ability to defeat any opponent through meticulous preparation and disciplined execution.

Historic upsets: Buster Douglas v Mike Tyson

My victory over Joppich parallels boxing's most astonishing upset, James 'Buster' Douglas defeating Mike Tyson in 1990. Tyson was considered invincible, dominating the heavyweight division with brutal knock-out power and speed. Douglas, motivated profoundly by the recent death of his mother, channelled this personal tragedy into meticulous, relentless preparation. He intensively studied Tyson's fighting style, identifying weaknesses in his defensive head movement and aggression.

Douglas fought patiently, carefully utilising his superior reach to frustrate Tyson's aggression and control the distance. As the fight progressed, Tyson became increasingly agitated and undisciplined, desperately swinging for the knock-out. Douglas maintained discipline, seizing his moment precisely in round 10 with a devastating combination, ultimately knocking Tyson out in a historic upset: strategic brilliance and psychological fortitude overcoming raw power and reputation.

Bonn World Cup 2017

The 2017 Bonn World Cup further solidified my belief. Over one remarkable weekend, I defeated five world-class fencers consecutively: Junhyuk Kwak (Korean Grand Prix medallist), Radoslaw Glonek (Polish, former world number two), Gerek Meinhardt (American, five-time

Olympian and world medallist), Alessandro Paroli (Italian, multiple World Cup medallist), and Erwan Le Péchoux (French, Olympic champion), eventually narrowly losing to Enzo Lefort (French, Olympic and two-time World Champion) in the quarter-finals.

The match against Meinhardt was particularly memorable. Meinhardt's technical mastery was legendary; at our respective peaks, he was undoubtedly superior. To win, I needed to shift dynamics. Two key factors shaped my strategy.

Firstly, Meinhardt hadn't fenced the previous day, receiving a bye due to his high ranking. While fresh, he lacked the intense competition sharpness I had gained fighting through the qualification rounds. Secondly, video analysis showed Meinhardt often started slowly, struggling initially to ignite his competitive spark. My strategy was clear: fence slowly, maintain a relaxed, low-intensity atmosphere and refrain from celebrations. Preventing him from finding emotional ignition was crucial. The strategy worked flawlessly.

Meinhardt never ignited his competitive fire, staying in first gear throughout. With calm precision, I executed my carefully prepared strategy scoring touches without celebrating and keeping the match at a low intensity. I secured a disciplined and controlled 15–11 victory.

Historic upsets: Leicester's Premiership

Leicester City's astonishing 2016 Premier League title mirrors my experiences in Bonn. Starting as 5000-to-1 outsiders, with relegation expected, Leicester meticulously created a disciplined, tactical strategy. Claudio Ranieri emphasised defensive organisation, leveraging players like N'Golo Kanté, Danny Drinkwater and Wes Morgan to form an almost impenetrable barrier. Offensively, Leicester relied on swift, incisive counterattacks through the lightning pace and precision of Jamie Vardy and creative brilliance of Riyad Mahrez.

As pressure intensified on favourites, Manchester City, Tottenham and Arsenal, they faltered under expectation. Leicester, free from expectation's burden, remained composed, ruthlessly executing their plan week by week, eventually clinching the title in a victory of tactical intelligence, psychological freedom and unyielding discipline; a classic testament to meticulous underdog preparation.

2018 World Championships

My draw for the round of 64 at the 2018 World Championships was Miles Chamley-Watson, a former world champion and Olympic medallist. Miles is a giant, standing 191 cm tall with an incredible wingspan. He's also one of the biggest personalities in fencing with a massive social media following. His technical ability was exceptional and his flashy hits often went viral online.

On paper, my task seemed impossible. He was over 20 cm taller, had a bigger reach and was technically superior. Yet nothing motivated me more than the chance to upset such a high-profile opponent.

Adding to the surreal atmosphere, Miles and I stayed in the same hotel, continually running into each other: at breakfast, in lifts, around every corner. The tension grew palpable. The night before our match, I discovered a promotional video he had done for Red Bull, jumping into ice baths, confronting fears. While others may have been intimidated, it motivated me further. My focus sharpened intensely onto my plan.

Aware of Miles's pressure for Olympic qualification, my tactic was clear: entice him into spectacular, high-risk moves. Although he scored some, each missed hit was my opportunity. The match unfolded precisely as planned. Miles missed many flashy points and, disciplined, I won 15–11.

Conclusion: the underdog's plan

These historical examples, as well my own experiences, only happened through meticulous preparation, deep understanding of opponent psychology, tactical flexibility and unwavering belief. These are the underdog's greatest strength. By clearly identifying your opponent's vulnerabilities and your own strengths, you define conditions for maximising your potential. It is about intention, clarity, discipline and resilience, not luck. Crafting and executing the underdog's plan transforms you from merely hoping to win into genuinely believing you will win, not just in fencing, but in any challenging aspect of life.

6

TEAM DYNAMICS

One thing I learned from my fencing career was that it was so much more fulfilling to win as a team than as an individual. When you win as a team, you share that victory with others who have worked alongside you. You've all experienced the same journey and, when it works, it's magical.

The years of fencing on the British team during my under-17 and under-20 days were magical. I was surrounded by team-mates who genuinely cared about me. They weren't just team-mates, they were friends, almost like brothers. We supported each other in all aspects of life: university lives, fencing careers and personal struggles. We won many international medals together and trained daily, but most importantly, we trusted each other. Those were truly great times.

For me, this is the ideal situation: your friends are your team-mates and you experience the journey together. However, life isn't perfect. My friends and brothers from those years had now left the sport of fencing and I was left with just team-mates.

You can compare the training environment to a workplace: you don't choose the people you work with, much like you don't choose your family. Many of us had trained together for over ten years. We knew each other well, spent more time with each other than with our own families and travelled the world together, but without fencing, we probably wouldn't have interacted.

The reality is you don't need to be best friends with your team-mates. The most important thing is goal alignment: having the same aim and agreeing on how to achieve it. I believe it's equally true for most workplaces and sports teams around the world. There are too many variables, too many egos and personalities, for everyone to get along perfectly.

Fencing brings a unique perspective to the concept of a team. We have two types of competition: individual and team. To make it into the team, you first have to compete against each other and only then are you selected to fence together as a four at events. After competing against each other in individual events, we had to pair up and support each other during team matches. It, of course, added another dimension to the relationships in the group, especially when vying for limited places.

Aligned like sisters

A prime example of a team that functioned like sisters is the US women's national soccer team, particularly during their victories at the Women's World Cup in 2015 and 2019. Players like Megan Rapinoe, Alex Morgan, and Carli Lloyd had played together for years, developing a deep bond that went beyond the field. They were friends, confidants and team-mates, creating a culture of trust and mutual respect. This unity was one of their key strengths and allowed them to dominate the world stage. Their shared journey, from training camps to world championships, built a connection that made playing together instinctive and seamless. The team's chemistry was a huge factor in their back-to-back World Cup wins.

The science behind such profound team chemistry is captured by research on collective efficacy, essentially, a team's shared belief in their ability to execute a specific task. According to Albert Bandura's social cognitive theory, collective efficacy is a strong predictor of group success. When team-mates trust each other's abilities and share a common goal, they tend to perform better, persist longer and handle pressure more effectively. This shared confidence is especially crucial in high-stakes situations, such as a World Cup final or Olympic qualification event.

Inaugural European champions

In 2015, I had qualified for the inaugural European championships as part of the British team. It was a proud moment to spend a day in Birmingham being kitted out with the rest of the athletes.

When it came to the individual event in Baku, however, all of us on the fencing team performed poorly. To make things worse, a journalist interviewed our star fencer, Richard Adam Kruse. For him, the upcoming world championships were more important and he was using this competition as preparation for that event. He explained that flying in the day before was not ideal for getting ready.

The next day, the headline in the *Evening Standard*, the London newspaper, read: 'Richard Kruse: we knew we would lose'. Our performance director called us in for a meeting and she was fuming. We got a 30-minute dressing-down about expectations, professionalism and our performance. We knew we were in the doghouse if we didn't improve.

The day after was the team event and our first match was the quarter-final against Germany, whom we dispatched comfortably. In the semi-finals, we were up against France, who, on paper, were much stronger than us. But as Aristotle (and later Richard Kruse) would say: 'the whole is greater than the sum of its parts'. We put in a great team performance and managed to cross the line, securing a place in the final. We were guaranteed a European medal, a pretty impressive feat.

During the break before the final, all the Team GB dignitaries had come to watch. We were told that the match would be broadcast live on British television. The final began and we were up against a strong Italian team led by Alessio Foconi, who had won gold in the individual event. They had just beaten the Russian first team, who would go on to win gold at the Rio Olympics.

The odds weren't in our favour, but with a medal already guaranteed, the pressure was off. My first bout went well: I defeated Foconi 5–1. My second match, against Nista, was a 10–7 loss, but we were still in the lead. Finally, I faced Ingargiola and suffered a 13–8 defeat, leaving us 35–33 down going into the final two legs with the match being played to 45 points.

A fantastic final two legs from Marcus and Richard propelled us to a 45–41 victory and we were crowned champions at the inaugural European Games. The podium was special, standing there, singing the national anthem while the Italians had to listen to us. It was a rarity, as the Italians win so much that I almost knew their national anthem by heart, having stood on the silver and bronze podiums listening to *Fratelli d'Italia* many times before.

Shared goals

The Chicago Bulls in the 1990s, led by Michael Jordan, were not necessarily a team of close friends off the basketball court. There were moments of tension between Jordan and his team-mates. Jordan was known for his relentless drive and competitive nature, which sometimes created friction within the team. However, what united them was their shared goal: to win championships. Under Jordan's leadership, the Bulls were able to win six NBA championships between 1991 and 1998.

In particular, Jordan's dynamic with Scottie Pippen stands out. While they weren't always best friends, they understood that their combined efforts were essential for the team's success. Their synergy on the court, despite occasional personal differences, was unstoppable. Their ability to put aside personal issues and focus on the shared objective exemplifies goal alignment leading to extraordinary success.

Research by organisational psychologist J. Richard Hackman underscores that it is the same for the rest of us: clearly defined shared goals serve as a unifying force, providing clarity and reducing internal conflict. Even teams with strong personalities and friction can thrive if each member clearly understands and aligns with the overarching mission. Hackman notes that successful teams often comprise individuals who may differ greatly in personality or background, yet become united and effective precisely because they commit deeply to a shared goal.

Team chemistry

Team chemistry, whether fuelled by friendship or professionalism, is vital. When goals are aligned, even teams that don't get along perfectly can reach great heights. For me, fencing was a mix of both. Sometimes, I had the privilege of competing alongside friends who felt like family. Other times, I had to push through with just team-mates, where our bond was based solely on the shared goal of winning. Both dynamics can work, but the important thing is that everyone is focused on the mission at hand. Ultimately, whether in sport or in any organisational setting, clearly articulated and collectively embraced goals forge unity. This goal alignment allows each team member to understand their role, recognise their value and commit wholeheartedly to something larger than themselves.

7

FIGHTING BACK

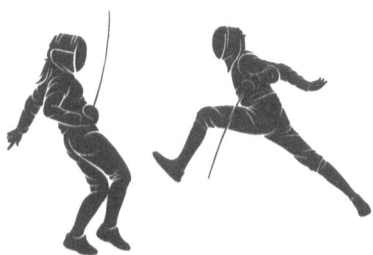

I entered the 2014-15 season ranked third in the British team, right in the mix for Olympic qualification. After finishing eighth in the World Championships team event in Kazan, my team-mates and I had a well-earned night out. It had been a long, intense year and we let off some steam in true fashion. But what lay ahead would make fencing results feel like a footnote.

Not long after, whispers began to spread that Lawrence Halsted, former team stalwart and Olympian, was planning a comeback in time for the Rio 2016 Games. If he returned anywhere near his old level, he'd be a strong contender for the third spot on the team. I brushed it off at first, saying, it's good competition. It was clear: only three would be selected based on rankings and the fourth spot was discretionary. The fight for places was about to intensify and I had no idea just how turbulent the season ahead would be.

On 27 May 2015, my father had travelled to Cyprus to help my grandfather (who was terminally ill with cancer) move from the hospital back home to spend his final months of life there. It had been a tough time for my Cypriot side of the family. My grandmother had passed away just a few months earlier and now my father was assisting with my grandfather's final days.

On 30 May 2015, I went to watch my football team, Arsenal, play in the FA Cup Final against Aston Villa. I was supposed to go with my mother, but our seats were rows apart and she never turned up. I messaged her, but she didn't respond. Arsenal comfortably won the cup, but something didn't feel right.

When I returned home, I received the devastating news that my father had suffered a heart attack at my grandfather's home and had passed away. I felt a wave of emotions: sadness, confusion, disbelief. There are moments that stay with you for life and this was one of them. I couldn't comprehend it: my grandfather was the one who was terminally ill. My father had been all smiles and in good spirits before he left for Cyprus. He passed away at the age of 57.

It was an incredibly difficult time for my family. I had just finished my exams and my sister was in the middle of her A-levels. For us, the world stopped. My father had been such a loving, caring presence, supporting me and my family in everything we pursued. It was hard to believe he would no longer be with us.

The funeral was arranged to take place in early June in Cyprus and we all went. The Cypriot way of grieving is very different from the British version. Funerals in Cyprus are cathartic, coming from the Greek word *katharizw*, meaning to clean or purify. The funeral is a deeply emotional event where all feelings are released to help cope with the loss.

One image that will forever scar me is seeing my dying grandfather, Andreas, being wheeled in to view my father's body. He was crying at the sight of his son. Herodotus once said that there is no worse fate than for a father to bury his son.

My father, Louis, was laid to rest in the family tomb, next to his mother, my grandmother. May they rest in peace.

After staying in Cyprus for a few days, I returned to London. I went straight back to training. I didn't process what had happened and instead returned to the only thing I knew how to do with my eyes closed: fencing.

Struggling to keep going

I returned to training, going through the motions. Ten days later, we set off for the inaugural European Games in Baku, Azerbaijan. There was a kitting-out day in Birmingham and it was fantastic to receive the kit and be among other Team GB athletes.

In the individual event, I just couldn't focus: my mind was elsewhere. I kept trying to compartmentalise my emotions and concentrate on fencing, but I was eliminated in the group stage, losing two matches 5–4, which meant I couldn't advance.

Mentally, I was in a tough place. Usually, I would be devastated by such a performance and being eliminated, but on that day I felt numb. I had lost my why. I had worked so hard to earn this opportunity and I deserved to enjoy it. However, the circumstances, emotions and feelings surrounding the death of my father prevented me from doing so.

A couple of months later the race for the four spots on the team for Rio continued with a world cup in the United States. I just wasn't getting the rub of the green. In the final match of direct elimination (round of 96), I lost 15–14, just missing out on advancing to the next day. That week of all weeks, after two months of intense training for the new season, I had come down with a throat infection. I powered through, but to lose 15–14 was devastating after giving everything I had. I actually started to cry. I didn't know how much longer I could keep this up.

The pink cherry trees of Tokyo

The season was relentless. Two weeks later, we were off to compete in the Tokyo World Cup. It was sink or swim. I had to get a result. That's the way you earned more freedom over your preparation and training before competitions. James Davis was ranked in the top 16 in the world and had had enough of the politics, so he decided to train in the US, which he was allowed to do because of his results. Richard Kruse was also in the top 16. They had the freedom to manage their own training, while the rest of us had to toe the party line.

When we arrived in Tokyo six days before the competition, it was decided that we must complete two gym sessions and two conditioning sessions, in addition to our technical training before the competition. It was something we had never done before, despite having travelled to many competitions across the world. We had our routines and it is ill-advised to change them at short notice, especially with no prior warning. A battle ensued and we were forced to comply or we would not be selected for the next competition.

By the day of the competition, I was demoralised, fatigued and lacking motivation. Emotionally drained from everything, I questioned why I was doing this at all.

I performed terribly in the poules. I didn't even care when I lost matches. Somehow, I managed to win two matches and lose four, finishing with an indicator (goal difference) of -6. Realistically, I was out. I didn't even take my kit off. I walked outside and saw the most memorable image.

Outside the hall was a park with a bench surrounded by the famous Japanese cherry trees. The ground was covered with blossoms and it was magical. I lay on the bench, looking up at the sky.

I was finished. I wasn't going to fence anymore. Life had caught up with me. I had decided I would quit the competition and quit fencing altogether. Everything had become too much: the loss in my family, combined with the negative environment within the fencing squad. I didn't have the mental capacity to continue.

Then, Amol Singh Rattan appeared. His name means 'priceless jewel' and that's exactly what he was. Having trained together since the age of 14, we had been on the same fantastic journey, almost like brothers. We motivated and helped each other, sharing in each other's successes and challenges. When I think of my fencing career, Amol is one of the top reasons for my success.

It is amazing in life to have someone with whom you can share such an experience. When one is down, the other provides a different perspective and you help each other rise. We rose through the ranks together, won many medals together and balanced fencing with academic pursuits.

Amol had recently earned a first-class degree from the London School of Economics and as a practising Sikh, he was devoting more time to his religious practices, often meditating for hours each day. I always felt safe travelling with him. If I was ever nervous about flying, having Amol next to me was settling. By the end of the year, he would leave the fencing world, but fortunately for me, he had stayed for one more competition in Tokyo.

As I lay on the bench, staring at the sky through the pink cherry blossoms, I heard a voice. 'Toff, Toff, where are you? Everyone is looking for you.' It was Amol. I replied, 'Amol, I'm done. I've had enough of fencing. I just want to go home.'

He responded, 'no, you were the last person to make it through'. I said, 'just tell coach Andrei to scratch me from the competition'. But then Amol said, 'you haven't heard the draw yet'.

Suddenly, my competitive drive burst through the fog. It turned out that I was matched against two fencers I had beaten before. My chimp (the impulsive, emotional part of the brain) was satisfied: I could win. My ego allowed me to participate.

I didn't fence them. I fought. It was pure fight or flight and I chose to fight. I dispatched both fencers with relative ease and made it through to the next day. The opponents who had been competing for the same spot didn't make it through.

Amol Singh Rattan had saved me and taught me the true value of friendship: to be there for someone not only in their best moments but in their darkest ones as well. It was a shame it was his last competition, but I was grateful for his support.

Finding inspiration at dark moments

My reward for making it through was a match against Yuki Ota of Japan, a two-time Olympic silver medallist and a national icon. It seemed as if Yuki alone was responsible for selling all the tickets. It was a full house, packed to watch us fence so early in the morning at 10am.

It was my favourite type of match-up: going against a top fencer with nothing to lose. The match started well for me. I was up 6–4, then

10–8 and finally 13–12. I was two hits away from an important result. Unfortunately, Yuki pulled it back and I lost 15–13.

By living through such dark moments, I found inspiration that motivated me to keep pushing toward my goals. It's in these challenging times, when everything seems to be falling apart, that we often find our greatest strengths. These moments force us to reflect, to fight for what truly matters and to uncover a deeper drive. Success isn't just about winning; it's about overcoming the internal battles and rediscovering the motivation to continue. It's in these moments that we often find the resilience to achieve our biggest dreams.

Fighting to the end

Time was ticking away and only three competitions remained. In the 2016 Paris World Cup, I battled into day two again. This time, in the round of 64, I was up against my team-mate, Richard Kruse. Drawing on my previous experience of fencing team-mates, I made my game plan and felt ready. The match went well, and with a minute remaining in the final period, the score was tied at 7–7. Unfortunately, I flinched first, missed an attack and started to chase Richard. It was ironic that a team-mate was putting one of the nails in the coffin of my Rio dream.

Then came the Bonn World Cup. I really had to make exceptional results in the remaining two competitions. Again, I fenced well on day one, progressing to day two. This time, I won my match in the round of 64, but once again, in the round of 32, I drew another team-mate, James Davis. It was another cagey match, neck and neck, as we reached 13–13, before James took the victory and went on to win the competition. Another nail in the coffin, hammered in by a team-mate.

With hope all but lost, we moved to the Grand Prix in Havana, where I competed on my birthday. Having made it again to the second day, I was defeated by Olympic silver medallist from London, Aladdin El-Sayed.

I shook hands, packed my bag, dropped it off at the hotel, took a taxi to Santa Maria Beach in Havana and jumped into the sea. I had fought until the last second and could have given no more.

I always remembered my father's words about finishing things until the end, irrespective of the outcome. I was competing in the Under-20 World Championships one year and was four hits behind with five seconds left, guaranteed to lose. I was about to salute and give up, but I remember my father shouting, 'Alex, it's not over… fight until the end'. I scored one more touch and still lost the match, but I have carried that attitude with me since and I will for the rest of my life. You keep fighting until the very end.

Not making Rio

The Team GB fencing team qualified for Rio, but I would not be part of it. Ultimately, I was unable to produce good enough results. Yes, there were many factors that made it difficult to perform, but in life, you get dealt a set of cards and you have to play them. I gave my best but failed; it was hard to take. At the time, it was also hard to see the personal growth I had experienced and the transferable skills I had learned in the process.

At that moment, I was physically, mentally and emotionally drained. I had been trapped in a negative, toxic environment within the fencing group while dealing with immense emotional stress. I needed an escape. I declined the offer to be the official reserve for Rio and decided to move to Egypt.

I was starting my master's degree at the London School of Economics in September and thought, what better way to distract myself from personal tragedies and the disappointment of not making the Olympics than by moving as far away as possible and learning a new language? I've always been a social person and learning languages opens doors. Even knowing a few words in someone's language makes them appreciative and helps build rapport.

The next chapter was waiting for me upon my return.

PART 2

8

TAKING RESPONSIBILITY

After returning to London from Egypt and reporting back to training, I was informed by the performance director of British Fencing, that I was no longer considered a prospect for the GB Olympic fencing team. She explained that the younger generation of athletes had greater potential, rendering me surplus to requirements, unfunded and facing uncertain selection prospects for future competitions.

During my time in Egypt, contemplating my future, I was deeply torn. My dream had always been to compete in the Olympic Games, yet I also longed for other experiences and achievements in life. The prospect of enduring another four years of fencing politics seemed daunting.

Unexpectedly, I received offers to fence for two different countries: Egypt and Cyprus. My father, Louis Andreas Tofalides, was born in Cyprus and moved to London for university, where he met my mother. As a person of mixed heritage, half British, half Cypriot, I often faced questions about my origins. In Britain, people would ask, 'but where are you originally from?' In Cyprus, I was viewed as British. This dual identity, though challenging, was ultimately enriching, instilling pride in both heritages.

Although Egypt offered an easier qualification pathway in the African zone and I could speak Arabic, I felt a deeper connection to Cyprus. After careful reflection, particularly following the conversation with the GB performance director, I decided to represent Cyprus. This decision was bittersweet; I had cherished the team camaraderie with GB, knowing I'd now face my fencing journey alone.

During my time fencing for Team GB, many of my responsibilities were managed for me. Flights, training schedules, strength and conditioning programmes, nutritional guidance, psychological support and fencing lessons were all carefully organised with specialists readily available and fully funded.

My transition to Cyprus forced me into an entirely new reality. No longer could I defer responsibility or assume someone else had the answers. I had to become my own performance director, coach, nutritionist and psychologist. This shift marked the start of a profound and transformative journey, one that would redefine my understanding of true accountability and self-reliance.

After nine fulfilling years with Team GB, highlighted by a gold medal at the European Games in Baku, I transitioned to Cyprus with their agreement.

A beginning with Cyprus

Initially, I was unsure what to expect. Cyprus had no foilists, my fencing discipline, only practitioners of epee, a distinctly different discipline. Cyprus also lacked experience with internationally competitive fencers. The technical director, Iraklis Emmanoulides, was a disciplined army man. Although his knowledge of high-level fencing was limited, his organisational skills, discipline and openness to learning laid a supportive foundation for me to gain a deeper understanding and practice of self-accountability.

Taking responsibility isn't merely about accepting blame or credit: it's fundamentally about acknowledging that the power to effect meaningful change lies primarily within yourself. Psychology tells us that humans naturally tend to externalise responsibility, especially under pressure or when faced with disappointment. It's comforting to believe our setbacks are caused by circumstances beyond our control, allowing us to deflect pressure, protect our self-esteem and avoid confronting uncomfortable truths.

In sport, as in life, the temptation to seek external solutions can be overwhelming. I fell deeply into this trap during my journey. For years, my mindset revolved around finding that one external factor, whether it be the perfect coach, the ideal training facility or better funding, that would unlock the success I desperately desired. I believed someone else held the key to my performance, overlooking the most critical element: myself.

Psychological research into accountability suggests that individuals who internalise responsibility are more likely to persist in the face of adversity, innovate solutions and achieve sustainable success. In contrast, those who habitually externalise blame or rely excessively on external solutions are less adaptable and more likely to repeat their mistakes, unable to learn from their experiences.

This concept played out vividly in my fencing career. One of the clearest signs of athletes looking externally for solutions can be seen during fencing matches: after every point lost, athletes instinctively turn their heads toward their coach, seeking answers, guidance or reassurance. It took me a long time to recognise how deeply ingrained this habit was within me and even longer to realise that the answers I sought from the sidelines often needed to be found within.

One stark example was the 2019 World Championships in Budapest. Obsessed with achieving the best possible result, I brought two coaches, convinced their combined expertise would provide the competitive edge I needed. However, their simultaneous advice overwhelmed me with nerves.

My mindset became fixated on results-based thinking: 'if I don't advance, it'll be disastrous'. Shifting back to a process-driven approach, which had previously brought success, felt impossible. Psychologically, habits and routines are incredibly challenging to alter quickly. Weeks of reinforcing a results-oriented mentality left me unable to redirect my focus under pressure, resulting in a crushing 15–11 defeat.

I was embarrassed and frustrated. I wanted to win so badly that I had sought external solutions, bringing an extra coach instead of focusing on the internal work I needed to do.

I had been searching for external stimulations to improve my performance, reach my goals and achieve results. But the bottom line was that to reach my goals, I needed to find the answers within myself. I had to take full responsibility for my actions and understand that I alone would be responsible for both success and failure. Unfortunately, it would take me a few more years to fully grasp this lesson.

External stimuli

In 2022, I attended the World Championships in Cairo, Egypt. This was the final World Championship before Olympic qualification kicked off again, offering an opportunity to secure a strong result without the same immense pressure that comes during Olympic qualifying. I was ready and motivated. However, my confidence in my coach, Ziemek Wojcieowski, had started to waver. While he was an excellent technician, I felt that he struggled to read the game in real-time during competitions.

I was still in a mindset of seeking external solutions rather than focusing on internal accountability. I hadn't yet fully embraced the idea that I needed to take more responsibility for my results. Seeing Alexander Choupenitch switch from Ziemek before the Tokyo Olympics, ultimately qualifying and winning a bronze medal, fed into this thinking. I was increasingly results-oriented and that quote, 'insanity is doing the same thing over and over again and expecting different results', kept echoing in my mind. It made me question whether a change in coaching was necessary for me too.

Similar patterns emerge across sports and business. Athletes often change coaches or teams repeatedly, believing new external influences will dramatically improve outcomes. A prime example in football is Manchester United following Sir Alex Ferguson's retirement in 2013. Ferguson had managed United for 26 years, building a culture of stability, internal development and long-term strategic planning, resulting in unprecedented success. However, in the decade following his departure, the club cycled through multiple high-profile managers, David Moyes, Louis van Gaal, José Mourinho, Ole Gunnar Solskjær and others, each promising rapid results. The frequent managerial changes disrupted team continuity and hindered long-term development. Ultimately, Manchester United's challenges illustrated clearly that enduring success requires stability, patience, internal growth and consistent responsibility, rather than continually seeking external quick fixes.

For six weeks before the World Championships, I returned to Frascati for training. There I encountered a unique opportunity. Andrea Baldini, Olympic and world champion, and one of my idols in the sport was coaching his wife, Irem Karamete. The chance to work with someone I held in such high esteem was too good to pass up. I believed that Baldini could provide the same psychological boost for me that Stefano Cerioni had provided for Choupenitch.

While training under Baldini did give me an immediate mental lift, learning from a legend of the sport, I quickly realised that he wasn't able to offer the kind of on-piste tactical coaching which I felt I needed due to his coaching another country at competitions.

So the World Championships arrived. On day one, I won five matches, losing just one. I had one elimination bout left to secure my spot for day two, which I won. My next opponent would be Danyil Hoida from Ukraine, a young fencer, and I was the clear favourite.

However, things didn't start smoothly. Hoida was relatively inexperienced and there wasn't the usual stockpile of footage I could review to fine-tune my strategy. I went into the match with a complacent mindset: 'I am the more experienced and better fencer; I will win'. This, of course, is the classic set-up for an upset.

The match began and it was hit for hit initially, but soon I found myself down 10–6. I remember turning around to look at Ziemek, hoping for a tactical lifeline, but he wore a blank expression. It was a look that told me I had to figure out the solution myself. Unfortunately, my brain wasn't firing on all cylinders. I rushed my points, made poor decisions, and before I knew it, I was out of the World Championships, losing 15–10 in the round of 64.

For me, it became crystal clear that continuing on the same path for another two years would be insanity, repeating the same process and expecting a different result, which in this case would likely mean not qualifying for the Olympics. After seven years with Ziemek, I had to make one of the toughest decisions of my career: changing coaches. Ziemek wasn't just my coach; he was 74 years old and had become a dear friend, someone I respected deeply.

Changing coaches wasn't a guaranteed path to success. That was the first thing I reminded myself. Yet, when faced with such pivotal decisions, I often picture myself at 70, sitting in my back garden in Cyprus, eating grapes and figs as the sun sets, reflecting on life. In those moments, I ask my older self, 'should I have done that or not?' And the answer is always the same: live life with no regrets. Take the chance. That way, I can never look back and wonder, 'what if?' The question now was: who would be my next coach?

In 2023 I attended the World Championships in Milan with a new coach again convinced that external coaching would give me the edge needed. However, after this competition, finally, I truly understood that only I could help myself. I was responsible for my preparation, my training and my performance on the piste.

Ben Peggs became my new coach. We had fenced together on the GB squad since the age of 13. He had now retired and become a coach. I had turned to someone who knew me and my fencing well and who, in the right moments I hoped, could deliver the right messaging.

Ben's coaching had certainly improved my in-competition support, but ultimately, the solutions to my challenges lay within me. For years, I had been searching for external stimuli, whether a coach, a new training environment or a tactical adjustment, to propel me toward my goals. But the truth was the best person to find those solutions had been staring back at me in the mirror all along. Moving forward, I knew I had to be brave, disciplined and honest with myself in taking responsibility for whatever unfolded in the next year.

Ben's role wasn't to find the answers for me, but to support me, to help push that proverbial rowing boat forward. All the while, I had been looking for someone else to steer, not realising that the captain of my ship had always been me.

The road to Luxembourg

After the 2023 World Championships, I took a much-needed break over the summer. My body was worn down and riddled with injuries, which is a common reality for athletes or anyone who trains intensely. To perform at the highest level, you must push your body through intense, repetitive training, often targeting the same muscle groups day after day. The physical toll becomes unavoidable and many athletes have their careers cut short by injury. The key is learning how to manage these issues, becoming a master of your own physiology, though even mastery doesn't always guarantee longevity..

Injuries highlight something deeply ingrained in human nature. We tend to ignore problems until they reach a critical point. Once they become unbearable, we seek out solutions, only to revert back to our old habits once the problem is fixed and the cycle starts again.

As for my recent hip injury, I thought it was improving after the World Championships, but the pain persisted. Running became impossible and I finally went to the doctor, who diagnosed me with inflammation of the hip joint, *osteitis pubis*. I would need to take six weeks off to recover.

In the end, this setback turned out to be a blessing in disguise. With a clear diagnosis, I could devise a structured plan for the road to Luxembourg. The goal was clear: I had to be in peak form for the zonal championships in April. Here was the roadmap:

- Mid-October to mid-November: a one-month physical conditioning programme to rebuild my strength and fitness.
- Mid-December to mid-January: focused technical training to sharpen my fencing skills.
- January and February: warm-up competitions in Paris and Turin to test myself in live matches.
- March: a three-week intensive training camp in Frascati, Italy, to push myself to the limit.
- April: the zonal championships in Luxembourg, the most critical event on the road to Paris 2024.

The stage was set.

Taking ownership

I knew that to be the best version of myself as an athlete, I needed to prioritise my health and take control of my situation. In the past, I had relied on painkillers to push through training, sometimes taking them twice a day for months on end. But I made a promise to myself that I would never rely on them again. I had to put my health first.

I had to confront some harsh realities. Staying in London due to my business, family and personal commitments meant I would be at a severe disadvantage compared to my competitors. With limited funding from the Cyprus Fencing Federation and limited time for camps or competitions, I had to ask myself: what can I do better than my competitors while training in London?

I identified three key areas: fitness, psychology, and video analysis. Through strength and conditioning, I could become stronger, more powerful and fitter than my opponents. Psychologically, I could master the art of compartmentalising other areas of my life during training or competition. And with video analysis, I could understand my opponents on and off the piste better than they understood themselves.

9

MENTAL PREPARATION

Success isn't built on isolated moments of brilliance: it's forged through the meticulous refinement of daily habits and processes. Over the course of my career, I developed a framework that allowed me to consistently perform at my best, whether in training, competition or recovery. These processes became second nature: preparing with my mental warm-up, structuring physical training for optimal performance and crafting tactical game plans tailored to each opponent.

In fencing, as in life, your greatest opponent is often not the person standing across from you, but the voice inside your head. Mental skills are not just a bonus in elite sport; they are the foundation. Fencing is a game of millimetres and milliseconds, where a single lapse in focus can cost you everything. It demands that you stay composed under pressure, adaptable in chaos and present in every second. The ability to master your mind, to silence doubt and stay anchored in the moment is what separates good athletes from great ones.

It is often referred to as being 'in the zone', a psychological state where thoughts and actions flow effortlessly, without hesitation or distraction. But this state doesn't happen by chance. It's built through disciplined mental training, just like physical conditioning. And the tools you use to thrive on the piste — focus, emotional regulation, self-belief — are the same tools that empower success in business, relationships and everyday life. Mastering your mind is the ultimate performance edge.

As I grew older, I realised that most of my stress didn't come from fencing itself but from external factors like business, family and life in general. When I stepped on the piste, I wasn't nervous anymore, but stress would build up outside of it.

Breathing first

I also incorporated a ten-minute box breathing exercise found in meditation to strengthen my ability to focus on the present moment.

- **Breathe in**: take a deep breath through your nose. Push your stomach out as you inhale.

- **Hold**: hold your breath for a few seconds.

- **Breathe out**: slowly exhale through your mouth.

- **Focus on thoughts**: let thoughts arise naturally. If your mind wanders, gently return focus to the breath.

- **Repeat**: continue for ten minutes to clear your mind and re-centre.

My mental warm-up

Step 1: addressing irrational emotional thoughts

Firstly, I would address and acknowledge any irrational, emotional thoughts I had. These might include self-doubt, such as worries about failure ('if I don't qualify, I'll be seen as a failure') or concerns about injuries I was carrying. I might also be distracted by personal or professional life pressures.

For each of these emotional concerns, I would pair it with a rational, logical response. For instance, to counter the fear of failure, I'd remind myself that success isn't always about the result, but about the effort and dedication I've put in. By rationalising these worries, I was able to manage and diminish their power over me.

Emotional thought	Logical response
'I'm feeling tired, how will I be able to fence today?'	'You've done the hard work: the training. Once you physically, mentally and technically warm up, you'll feel ready.'
'I have to win all my matches in the group.'	'With this mentality, you won't win any. Focus on the controllables: your process for each point gives you the best possible chance.'
'I have so much work to do.'	'Nothing that happens now will affect your work. You've earned the right to focus on your fencing, so do it.'

Step 2: building confidence

Once I'd addressed the emotional noise, I'd shift focus to building up my confidence. I'd remind myself of the thousands of hours of training I'd put in over my 21-year fencing career and that I had more than 10,000 hours of experience, making me an expert and world-class fencer.

Then I'd think back to a specific moment when I fenced exceptionally well. I'd reflect on how it felt, how well I executed my preparation and how I followed through with my tactical plan. This memory served as a reminder of what I was capable of when I stuck to my processes.

Finally, I would remind myself: if I am physically, technically and mentally ready, I will fence my best. That meant:

- Good mental warm-up (ten minutes breathing in the taxi).
- Good physical warm-up: foam roll, active warm-up, tape knee.
- Good technical lesson.
- Good sparring.
- Good footwork before the bout.

Step 3: strengths and trigger cues

Next, I would go through my physical, technical and tactical strengths, applying trigger words or cues to access those qualities during competition.

MENTAL PREPARATION

	Strength	**Cue**
Physical	'You are fit and strong. You have good footwork. You fence your best when you manoeuvre your opponent up and down the piste.'	'Movveeeeee' (hand sign – moving in and out).
Tactical	'You are sharp when executing each touch with a clear purpose.'	'Small first step, know where you're going to finish.'
	Attack	**Defence**
Technical: plan A	• Two-wave press finish with blade, step-lunge. • Great attack-counter riposte. • Strong attack remise. • Forward press counter-time finish. • Excellent manoeuvring in and out while attacking.	• Fake proving of parries. • Fake counterattack into parry riposte (nb, balanced step on feint). • Very good beat-the-blade to initiate attack. • Manoeuvring defence using in-and-out footwork: make opponent uneasy.

Step 4: plan B in the middle game

If my plan A wasn't working, I would adopt my Plan B or its variation.

Plan Bs	Cues
If need to go straight off the line, play the Wheel of 4: a) Step, step, lunge; b) Step, step, disengage lunge; c) Step, step, in parry-riposte (arm must be active on first step: no searching); nb, arm out if going for direct.	'Tactical wheel middle'
Pause first step to get opponent to react first. Then either step in for parry-riposte or take initiative.	'Middle pause'

Step 5: affirmation, owning the moment

At this point, I would close the mental warm-up with a final affirmation: 'You've done all the preparation, mentally, physically and technically. You've earned the right to be here. Stay in the moment. Let go of outcome. Trust the process. Fence with freedom and enjoy the fight'.

Step 6: opponent-specific tactics

If I am competing in a major event, I'll also incorporate specific tactical plans for each likely opponent. Here's an example of how I prepared for the Turin World Cup.

MENTAL PREPARATION

Opponent	Plan A	Plan B
Yeung Chi Ka (Hong Kong)	Close quarters parry stepping forward in the middle of the piste.	Short pressure steps, provoke with blade actions, finishing with lunge.
Khalifa Abdulla (Qatar)	Use beats to draw out counterattack.	Strong step-step attack off the line.
Wong Adam (Canada)	Take initiative, finish attack when he counters.	Use the whole piste, draw out his attack to finish with parry riposte.
Gross Roy (Israel)	Take initiative, make attacks with the blade.	Pushing forward, make him react and finish with counter-time attack.
Oursler Charles (US)	First intention attacks. He commits early, arm first attacks.	Deep defence, second-intention set-ups.
Minott Kamal (GB)	Establish dominance. Press and provoke with speed.	Use the whole piste, defend with distance to restart your attacks.

Compartmentalisation: creating space to compete

The skill of compartmentalisation became invaluable during this time. I dedicated each part of my day to a specific aspect of my life, whether it was training, work or personal matters. If certain tasks could be delegated, I entrusted them to others, and I always started my day with a mental warm-up. Before training, my mind would often be crowded with thoughts and concerns from different areas of my life, but by the end of my mental warm-up, I was ready to focus on fencing.

The key was applying logic to my emotional concerns. I reminded myself that the time I was spending training, whether for two or three hours, was strictly for fencing. Worrying about other matters during training wouldn't change anything, so I refocused my mind on my specific training goals. This approach helped clear my head and prepare me mentally for the task at hand.

However, there were still moments when intrusive thoughts would pop into my head while I was working on something else. In those instances, I first acknowledged the thought, applied logic to it and, if that didn't calm my emotional side, I turned to my breathing exercises. I would breathe in deeply, pushing out my stomach, hold my breath and then exhale through my mouth, refocusing on the breath each time another thought surfaced. This technique, which I had practised many times, allowed me to regain control and stay on course.

While it's essential to deal with personal concerns, sometimes there isn't time to dive deep into every thought. In those moments, applying logic and using breathing exercises helped me stay focused, especially during the intense months leading up to the Olympic qualification.

10

PROCESS AND ROUTINE

Routine is the key to success. Of course, by routine, I mean successful routines. As Aristotle once said, 'we are what we repeatedly do. Excellence, then, is not an act, but a habit'. Human beings are driven by routines. We follow the tried and tested. If something works, we do it again. This principle extends to all areas of life. Day to day, we develop routines for everything: from how we brush our teeth in the morning to how we complete our work or even the way we exercise.

For athletes, this process is no different. Throughout our careers, we aim to perfect our routines. When you succeed in a competition, you reflect on what worked. Was your warm-up routine effective? Were your tactics right? Did you sleep well the night before? Did you eat well during the competition?

Likewise, when you don't perform as well as you hoped, you analyse what went wrong. Maybe you overtrained or perhaps you ate too much before competing. There are countless factors that can affect performance and it takes a long time to get it right. Some may never reach that sweet spot.

The learning process

It's impossible to rush this process because success depends on your ability to accurately analyse situations. If you misinterpret the data, you can end up embedding false routines into your mind, which you think work but actually don't, or dismissing routines that could be successful. As Albert Einstein famously said, 'insanity is doing the same thing over and over and expecting different results'.

The bottom line is that to discover and ingrain successful routines, you need to fail a lot. Failure teaches you valuable lessons, provided you can correctly interpret those failures.

Stage 1: accurately analyse the situation

Many people fail at this first stage. The problem with failing here is that it's much harder to unlearn something and then relearn it, than to learn something new from scratch.

Stage 2: understand what needs to be learned

This analytical skill can be practised over time. It's difficult to hone under pressure, but with enough experience and a well-developed process, it becomes manageable.

Stage 3: implement the lesson

This is the hardest part, knowing the lesson you've learned but struggling to implement it. The mind can get in the way here, much like the chimp model popularised by Steve Peters. However, let's call it the reaction brain to keep it more understandable. Your reaction brain works in the background, driving impulsive decisions, while your logical mind must override it. Under pressure, the reaction brain may cling to old, familiar habits, even when you consciously know better.

Performing under pressure

Life is a constant process of forming, reforming and refining our routines and patterns. We are shaped by our life experiences and, when it comes to performance, our brains will always make decisions based on the patterns and routines most deeply wired. These routines are based on past experiences and perceived successes.

This understanding is crucial when analysing opponents. We used video to break down the actions and points scored by opponents, especially under stress. In fencing knock-out matches, the score is first to 15, but the moment of highest pressure is often at 14–14. This is the ultimate fight-or-flight situation. You face two paths: one leads to victory, the other to defeat. At that moment, all the work you've done, all the great points you've scored, no longer matters.

Your mind drifts to the future: what will it feel like if I win? What will happen if I lose? Our minds constantly wander into the past and into the future, and we often struggle to pull them back into the present. But in high-pressure moments, the ability to analyse the present accurately is key. Sometimes, under pressure, you won't be able to think through every detail and you will have to rely on the routines you've built.

At 14–14, you may have only three to five seconds to think before the final point. In that short window, there isn't enough time for deep analysis. Your brain relies on the routines you've programmed into it. The difficulty is not so much in knowing what to do as in doing it.

The pressure cooker of 14-14 brings out those ingrained routines. Over a career, a fencer will face many such moments. You'll build a huge mental dataset of what worked and what didn't, sometimes even specific to certain opponents. When the lights are on and the pressure is high, you revert to what you are most comfortable with and what you believe gives you the best chance of success.

When our video analyst reviewed the data, we saw that many fencers had a go-to move in high-pressure situations. This showed me a powerful truth about human nature: we gravitate towards the familiar. The key is to ensure that you've programmed the right routines into your brain, based on accurate interpretations of past experiences.

Control the controllables

In fencing, as in life, there are many things outside of your control. You can't dictate whether you'll win or lose, control the actions and emotions of others, or predict unexpected events.

In everyday life, the uncontrollables are all around us. You might hit unexpected traffic on the way to a crucial job interview. Your boss might come into work in a bad mood, changing the tone of your entire day. A sudden illness could throw off weeks of careful planning. Even something as small as your train being delayed or your child waking up sick can completely derail your schedule. These moments often provoke strong emotional responses: frustration, anxiety, disappointment or even a sense of helplessness. What makes uncontrollables so difficult is that they strike without warning and remind us that, no matter how prepared we feel, there are always factors we can't influence.

However, what you can control is how you manage your own emotions, how you react to different situations and how well prepared you are for the challenges ahead. The key is first accepting that not everything will be in your control and that's okay. Once you release the pressure of trying to control the uncontrollable, you can shift your focus fully to what's within your power. This is what it means to control the controllables, a concept that applies far beyond sport.

It might mean setting your alarm early, preparing your outfit and transport the night before, doing the best possible job with the information and tools you have, and showing up with the right mindset. It doesn't guarantee the outcome, but it gives you the best possible shot and that's all anyone can do.

My approach to the zonal qualifier for the Olympics in Luxembourg was based on a twofold strategy: first, I focused on controlling the controllables; second, I prepared myself to manage my emotions when uncontrollable events occurred.

From September 2023, I planned backwards from the date of the competition, 26 April 2024, so that my training, professional commitments and personal life would all align with that one moment. My training was meticulously organised, targeting technical, mental and physical improvements. Professionally, I ensured that by April, I would step back from work, becoming unreachable a week before the event, to allow full focus on my preparation.

By February 2024, I had booked flights, hotels and made all logistical arrangements for my coach and physio. My sister kindly took on the task of organising travel and accommodation for my support team, family and friends who would be there to cheer me on.

A month before I went to the training camp in Frascati, I had my competition kit and nutritional supplements ready. Everything from protein shakes to energy drinks was organised. I also mapped out the final week in minute detail, right down to the moment I would board the plane to Luxembourg. This gave me the psychological confidence of ticking off each controllable, one by one. With each completed task, my readiness for the competition felt more certain.

Preparing for the entire journey

One significant adjustment I made was in how I approached preparation. In the past, I had focused only on specific milestones, getting through day one, then preparing for day two. This often left me falling short because I hadn't fully prepared for the entirety of the event. For example, I might win the first match on day two but lose the next, as I wasn't fully equipped physically, mentally or nutritionally for the whole competition. This time, I prepared as though I was going to win the entire tournament. I adopted a mindset that encompassed everything, each day, each round and every possible scenario.

11

PSYCHOLOGICALLY AWARE

Psychological awareness is one of the most powerful tools you can possess in life, sport and personal growth. It is the ability to understand your own emotions, motivations and mental state, and how these elements interact with your environment and influence your decisions. When you become psychologically aware, you develop clarity about your strengths, vulnerabilities and tendencies under pressure. You begin to recognise that the greatest battles often occur within your own mind. Mastering psychological awareness means equipping yourself with the tools to navigate challenges and seize opportunities, no matter how unpredictable or difficult circumstances become.

The stone of life

In *The Chimp Paradox*, the sport psychologist Steve Peters introduces the stone of life as a personal reference point comprising three key elements:

- **Truths of life**: these are fundamental beliefs about how the world operates. Recognising and accepting these truths can provide emotional stability.

- **Values**: these represent your core principles and ideals, guiding your behaviour and decisions.

- **Life force**: this reflects your overarching purpose or philosophy in life. It's the essence of what you believe life is about and how it should be lived.

Understanding these cornerstones of your life and identifying your core values is foundational to psychological awareness. These cornerstones act as guiding principles or essential truths, reminders that help ground you during turbulent times. These principles reflect universal truths that help us cope, thrive and make sense of life's complexities. When internalised, these cornerstones can significantly enhance your emotional resilience, decision-making and sense of fulfilment.

Ten cornerstones

So what cornerstones could I draw from my own life experiences to collectively form a robust framework to strengthen my psychological awareness, resilience and effectiveness. For me, there were ten:

- **Life is unfair**: recognise that unfairness is an inherent part of life. Accepting this truth frees you from unnecessary resentment or frustration, empowering you to respond constructively rather than reactively.

- A **quarter of people won't like you**: no matter how hard you try, some people simply won't resonate with you and that's okay.

Accepting this reduces the stress of seeking universal approval and helps you focus on authentic relationships.

- **Only you truly understand yourself**: ultimately, you alone fully grasp your inner world, motivations and feelings. External validation can guide you, but genuine fulfilment and success come from internal clarity and authenticity.

- **Focus your mind on the present**: mastering present-moment awareness frees you from anxiety about the future and regrets of the past. This mindfulness anchors you in actionable reality.

- **Forgiveness liberates you**: holding onto grudges burdens your emotional wellbeing more than it harms others. Forgiving is a practice of emotional intelligence that restores your mental and physical energy.

- **Put life into context**: every setback or disappointment must be viewed within the broader context of life's bigger picture. This perspective fosters gratitude, reduces emotional volatility and promotes long-term resilience.

- **External factors will always exist**: understand and accept that many aspects of life lie outside your control. What you can manage, however, is your response. This cornerstone helps maintain composure under pressure.

- **Process over outcome**: outcomes are never guaranteed, no matter the effort or intention. By shifting your focus to the process, the habits, routines and methods you employ, you maximise your potential for success.

- **Take full responsibility for your life**: complete ownership of your actions, decisions and their consequences places you in the driver's seat. This accountability is both empowering and necessary for authentic progress.

- **Enjoy the journey**: ultimately, finding joy and meaning in the pursuit, not just in outcomes, sustains motivation, enhances performance and enriches life. Remembering why you started your journey often provides the most profound psychological fulfilment.

While these are the ten that have guided me, everyone is free to reflect and define their own. When you embrace your personal cornerstones, you can navigate life's complexities with clarity, purpose and a deeper understanding of yourself, as well as strengthening your psychological awareness, resilience and effectiveness in life.

Self-awareness

Developing self-awareness has been a pivotal element in my personal and athletic growth. It involves deeply understanding your strengths and weaknesses, maintaining the discipline to continually refine your processes, and cultivating resilience to persist regardless of obstacles.

Of all the lessons I've learned, the most critical is the importance of truly knowing yourself. In the end, no coach, family member or friend can take responsibility for your life's outcomes: this responsibility lies solely with you. Recognising and accepting your strengths and weaknesses, learning from every experience, and continuously adjusting your approach is fundamental to sustained growth.

Self-awareness is the key to unlocking your potential. Without it, you remain vulnerable to external influences that can derail your focus or diminish your capabilities. Mastery of self-awareness, particularly the ability to maintain composure and make effective decisions under pressure, can be developed through dedicated training, visualisation exercises and deliberate scenario planning.

Scenario planning

Scenario planning is a powerful psychological tool that involves anticipating various situations and mentally rehearsing your responses. By preparing for multiple potential outcomes, you develop greater flexibility, composure and decision-making ability under stress. This proactive approach equips you to handle unexpected events calmly and effectively, minimising anxiety and enhancing your performance, both in sports and everyday life.

Fencing scenarios	Positive reaction
Referee makes a questionable call.	Politely ask for clarification, remain calm and adapt tactics.
Feeling physically unwell or fatigued.	Recall past competitions when you performed despite illness; remind yourself of your proven processes to get in the zone.
Opponent scores three touches in quick succession.	Take a deliberate break, tie shoelaces or adjust equipment; use this time to reassess tactics calmly and refocus.
Distracting thoughts about personal or business matters.	Gently acknowledge the thought, remind yourself it can wait and redirect your full attention back to fencing.

Effective scenario planning involves two core steps: writing out potential scenarios with corresponding positive reactions and then reinforcing these reactions through visualisation. First, identify possible situations you might encounter and determine how you would ideally respond to each. Writing these down helps clarify your strategy and reinforces your cognitive preparedness.

Once scenarios are outlined, visualisation deepens your preparation. Sit quietly and vividly imagine yourself experiencing each scenario, carefully moving through each action and emotional response. Picture yourself on the fencing piste or in your own situation, handling the scenario with confidence and poise.

Scenarios in life	Positive reaction
Facing unexpected criticism at work.	Listen objectively, acknowledge valid points calmly and suggest constructive solutions.
Anxiety before an important public speaking event.	Recall previous successful speaking experiences, practise breathing techniques and visualise delivering your speech confidently.
Conflict with a friend or family member.	Pause before responding, remind yourself to listen actively, and approach the conversation with empathy and openness.
Sudden unexpected delay in your daily schedule.	Acknowledge the frustration briefly, then calmly reorganise your priorities to efficiently manage the time available.

The more detailed and realistic your visualisation, the more effectively your mind internalises these responses. Although it's impossible to anticipate every eventuality, practising this regularly creates a mental database of effective reactions that you can instinctively draw upon when needed.

Switching to plan B

Three years before qualifying for the Paris Olympics, I competed in Madrid at the European qualifier for the Tokyo Olympics. I had made it to the quarter-finals and standing opposite me was Michal Siess, a World Championship finalist. Tall and athletic, he had a height advantage of at least 15 centimetres over me and would be a formidable hurdle to overcome. In preparation I had devised two game plans.

Plan A was to absorb his attacks and score with defensive actions at my end of the piste. Michal and I had both been training at the same club in Italy in the months leading up to the event and this strategy had worked well in our practice bouts, so I decided to start with it.

When the match began I put plan A into action, but within 30 seconds I was trailing 2–0. Michal scored two clean hits with ease. This is where all the work I had put into scenario planning would be put into action. I had set myself a rule that if I lost two points in quick succession I would take a break (in this case I bent down to tie my shoelace), using that moment to assess whether the tactics were wrong and needed changing or if it was simply my execution that needed adjusting.

Because I had rehearsed this kind of decision-making both in training and through visualisation, I was able to stay calm under pressure and make the right call: the tactics had to change and plan B put into effect. Immediately, I switched to the offensive. On this day, the best defence was attack. I surged forward, pressing him with a series of aggressive actions. Caught off guard, Michal couldn't respond to the shift in momentum and I managed to turn the bout around winning 15–11.

12

DATA ANALYSIS

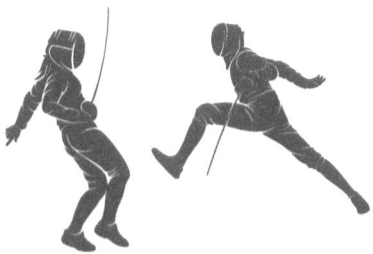

In high-performance sport, analysis is everything. Without it, you are operating in the dark, relying on hope rather than knowledge. But the most critical mistake many athletes make is thinking that analysis begins with studying others. It doesn't. The first opponent you must master is yourself.

Before video analysis, before opponent scouting, before tactical breakdowns, true growth starts with an honest, forensic examination of your own strengths, weaknesses, habits and mental tendencies. No amount of opponent analysis can save you if you aren't first crystal clear about your own patterns under pressure.

In fencing and in life, the more you understand yourself, the more effectively you can execute under stress. Self-analysis teaches you how you respond in key moments: whether you stick to your plan, how you handle adversity and where your habits tend to break down. It is only through this brutally honest internal assessment that you can build strategies that truly work, both for your style and your psychology.

Once you have built this foundation, then, and only then, does external analysis come into its true power. Studying opponents becomes a way to layer specific tactics on top of your rock-solid internal game. It's an extension, not a replacement. Opponent analysis shows you how to adjust your execution to exploit their weaknesses, but it never replaces the core work of knowing yourself.

Video analysis became a critical tool for both of these processes. First, to refine my own routines, strategies and reactions under pressure. Second, to uncover predictable patterns in my opponents, especially their behaviours at critical moments like 14–14 or when under immense pressure. Human beings are creatures of habit and data is key in fencing, as it is in many other fields. In moments of stress, people tend to repeat the same successful actions or the same mistakes.

Under the radar

In the lead-up to the zonal qualifier, I made a key decision: I would not participate in all the remaining competitions before the event. Despite having finished second at the previous zonal qualifier, no one was counting on me to win this one. During training sessions and competitions, all the talk centred around who the current favourites were based on recent results.

I realised I was slipping under the radar and, for the first time, I was glad. It gave me the freedom to focus solely on my unique training and preparation. I was learning that it wasn't about being the favourite; it was about finding and executing the right formula when it mattered most.

DATA ANALYSIS

Preparation for the zonal

After the Turin Grand Prix in February, I spent the next eight weeks focusing intensely on my technical and tactical strategy for the zonal. The key was to refine and perfect my plan A.

Fencing had evolved significantly in recent years, favouring taller fencers and those on the attack. In foil fencing, whoever initiates the attack usually gains the advantage. Many fencers had adopted the technique of advancing with their arms held back to avoid early engagement, forcing defenders to expend much more energy to counter. I knew that defending was far more exhausting than attacking and this insight led me to commit fully to a more aggressive, forward-focused style.

My entire strategy was built around dominating the centre of the piste and controlling the match through relentless attacks. I made the decision to spend the next two months honing this approach in every training match, believing that if I practised it a thousand times while my opponents practised it a hundred times, it would give me the edge. I was prepared to live or die by this strategy.

A coordinated approach

I relayed this strategy to my coach, Ben Peggs, who incorporated it into every training session. Each lesson was built around reinforcing my tactics, embedding them so deeply that they became second nature.

I also spoke with my physio, Maria Goirup, who adjusted my strength and conditioning programme to align with this more aggressive, physically demanding approach. Every aspect of my preparation was now coordinated to support the same central plan.

Finally, I collaborated with Raffi Rhys Pollitt, my sparring partner and video analyst, to simulate real match conditions. Most days, I trained with Raffi at the Lansdowne Club. He was a talented British fencer with a strong ability to control the middle of the piste and attack effectively, making him the perfect training partner for sharpening my strategy.

Our matches were intense, competitive and often aggressive. He knew my tactics, which made the training even harder for me, but that was exactly what I needed. Losing matches in training meant I was learning. It forced me to sharpen my focus and prepare myself mentally and physically for the zonal.

Over those eight weeks, I lost more training matches than I won, but I was willing to endure this because I knew it was the key to being ready when it mattered most. The idea was simple: refine my tactics through relentless practice so that, when the time came, I would be ready to impose my style on anyone I faced at the zonal qualifier.

The opponent database

Around this time, we embarked on a crucial project that would become the final piece in my preparation for the zonal qualifier: creating a comprehensive database of all the fencers who would be competing.

There were about 25 to 30 potential competitors and we had confirmed around 80 percent of them. We began by studying videos of these opponents, focusing specifically on their matches against fencers similar to me, left-handed athletes with comparable body types. The goal was to analyse how my plan A (aggressive forward fencing) would match up against their habits and whether any adjustments would be necessary.

This tactical study didn't stop at general fencing styles. We broke down specific technical points, such as:

- Where I should aim my attacks.
- Which target areas were most vulnerable.
- The optimal piste positioning to execute these actions.

For instance, certain fencers were far more vulnerable when pushed toward the end of the piste, while others struggled when forced to engage at the centre.

But my favourite part was analysing the psychology of each opponent. I wanted to understand any mental cracks or weaknesses they might have:

- Did they lose composure when arguing with referees?
- Did they get flustered under pressure?
- Did they struggle with fatigue late in matches?
- Did they dislike aggressive fencers who beat the blade?
- Were they thrown off by unorthodox or unpredictable tactics?

These psychological insights allowed me to build narratives in my head, giving me that extra mental edge going into a match. By the time the zonal competition approached, we had built a comprehensive database filled with tactical strategies, technical breakdowns and psychological profiles for each potential opponent. This knowledge would be critical in formulating specific strategies for every match, ensuring that I had a clear plan for anyone I might face.

13

TRAINING AND SPARRING

If there's one universal truth in sport or in any pursuit of excellence, it's this: training is everything. It is the bedrock of every great achievement. No title, no medal, no breakthrough moment happens without it. The hours you put in when no one's watching, those quiet, unglamorous, disciplined repetitions, form the invisible scaffolding of success.

Whether in sport, business or creative work, the quality of your training determines the quality of your performance. You can't control the outcome of every match or project, but you can control your preparation. You can choose how much time, focus and intentionality you bring to your training, day in, day out.

This is where the concept of 10,000 hours becomes relevant. Popularised by Malcolm Gladwell (and grounded in research by Anders Ericsson), it suggests that achieving mastery in any field requires 10,000 hours of deliberate practice. But it's not just about clocking hours. It's about how you train. Mindless repetition doesn't build greatness; purposeful, focused, feedback-driven effort does.

Yet, even in elite circles, a dangerous trap exists: the belief that training more – longer, harder, with greater intensity – will automatically lead to improvement. When we feel behind or insecure, we instinctively try to catch up by doing more. But this can be counterproductive. Without structure, purpose or recovery, more training can lead to burn-out, injury or plateau.

What really matters is your ability to train the right way, not harder, but smarter. That means focusing on your process, not obsessing over results. It means cultivating the habits, routines and mindset that support sustainable growth. It means knowing your body, your psychology and what kind of environment brings out your best.

Training is non-negotiable. Everyone at the top puts in the hours. But what separates champions from the rest isn't just how much they train: it's how they train, how they think and how they adapt.

This chapter is about everything I learned during those thousands of hours on the piste and in the gym: the environments that shaped me, the sparring partners who sharpened me, the mentors who challenged me and the routines that allowed me to evolve from a teenage fencer with talent into an Olympic athlete. It's about the craft of training and how to make it work for you.

Environment is everything

By the age of 13, I had the good fortune of joining Salle Paul, based at William Ellis School in Highgate. The significance of this location cannot be overstated: it was a two-minute drive or a ten-minute walk from my house. But more than just convenience, it became my gateway to elite training.

Salle Paul housed two incredible coaches, Ziemek Wojcieowski and Maciej Wojtowiak, senior and junior coaches of Team GB. The quality of coaching was world class, but it was the proximity that made it possible for me to immerse myself in that level of training consistently. I was lucky. As Matthew Syed explores in *Bounce*, proximity to opportunity is one of the most overlooked factors in success. He highlights how many high performers, whether in sport, music or business, benefitted from simply being born near the right coaches, clubs or facilities.

That was true in my case. Without Salle Paul on my doorstep, I may never have had regular access to the kind of training that propelled me to Olympic qualification years later. Syed argues that while talent and hard work are critical, environment amplifies both and when you add opportunity into the mix, the results can be transformative.

Over the course of my career, I trained in many different environments, each shaping me in unique ways. From the high-performance pressure cooker of the GB performance programme, the international intensity of Frascati in Italy to the Leon Paul Centre in London after the end of my GB career and, later, the solo focus of my self-directed routine at the Lansdowne Club prior to the Paris Olympics. What I learned is this: in elite sport, your environment is just as important as your mindset or skill set.

The right environment shapes everything: your energy, your expectations, your level. If the people around you are pushing for excellence, you rise to meet them. If they're coasting, you might unconsciously lower your own standard. Culture is contagious.

A great parallel comes from the world of football. Sir Alex Ferguson, the legendary manager of Manchester United, was known not just for his tactical brilliance, but for his ability to create a winning environment. His outlook was simple: hard work will always overcome natural talent when natural talent does not work hard enough.

At Manchester United, excellence wasn't optional: it was expected. From the newest academy players to global superstars like David Beckham, every individual had to buy into the culture of relentless work ethic, focus and team-first mentality. Those who didn't were quickly sidelined, regardless of talent.

That same principle applied across every training environment I've thrived in. In Frascati, for example, training with Olympic champion Daniele Garozzo and other top-tier athletes, the intensity was non-negotiable. You didn't show up to go through the motions; you showed up to get better. Every session was a test. Every bout was a battle. But within that, we were sharpening each other, feeding off each other's hunger.

After the British programme collapsed, the Leon Paul Fencing Centre became a hub for international training between 2016 and 2020. It was a rare opportunity to fence with world-class athletes from multiple countries, Hungary, Ukraine and Hong Kong, and to continue training daily with Richard Kruse, one of the world's best. That environment kept me sharp during a transitional time, right up until the Tokyo Olympic cycle.

However after this training group disintegrated in 2021, I was left with fewer sparring options, I built a more self-reliant structure at the Lansdowne Club. Though the set-up was different, less international, more individually focused, it taught me how to take full ownership of my development. I created my own structure, controlled my own intensity and pushed myself harder than anyone else could.

Across all of these environments, the same rule applied: you are only ever as good as the environment you immerse yourself in. And if the environment doesn't exist, you build it. You bring in partners. You raise the bar. You take full responsibility for the energy in the room.

In sport, business or any high-performance field, success isn't just about talent or effort. It's about building or finding the right setting to grow. The right environment fuels the habits, standards and mindset that lead to greatness. Once you experience that kind of setting, you'll never settle for anything less.

Building a high-performance routine

After the World Championships in Milan 2023, I knew it was time to take full responsibility for every aspect of my performance, physical, technical and psychological. Without regular access to world-class sparring partners, I had to adapt if I was going to have a shot at qualifying for the Olympic Games. The challenge now wasn't just about refining my skills, but about building the right training environment from the ground up.

I moved my training base to the Lansdowne Club in Mayfair, a place that held personal significance. It was where I had trained with the British team in the lead-up to the London Olympics and it housed one of the only permanent fencing salles in central London. I turned that salle into my performance hub for the next nine months.

My daily routine at Lansdowne followed a deliberate rhythm. Mornings were dedicated to fencing and technical work, followed by mental preparation and psychological training, which included breathing exercises, visualisation, tactical planning and my structured mental warm-up. After that, I would work in the club's business centre until 5pm, followed by a gym session and recovery work before heading home. This structure gave me consistency and clarity. It eliminated distractions. I finished both work and training by 6:30pm, giving me balance and allowing me to focus fully when it mattered.

By consciously building in psychological work, rather than treating it as an optional extra, I ensured I was preparing the complete athlete: physically strong, technically sharp and mentally resilient.

I also began inviting one or two select sparring partners for private, high-intensity sessions. The salle could get hot, suffocatingly so at times, but that discomfort became an asset. It toughened me. These sessions weren't about numbers: they were about intensity, execution and conditioning. In the absence of a full squad, I created my own micro-environment: competitive, deliberate and focused. Every touch had to matter. Every session had to move the boat forward.

It was a stark reminder that success is rarely about perfect conditions. It's about how you respond when things aren't ideal. I couldn't replicate the depth of sparring I once had, but I could ensure every session was purposeful. That mindset shift from 'what am I missing?' to 'what can I maximise?' became one of the most powerful tools in my arsenal.

14

NEGATIVE THOUGHTS

Negative thoughts can derail even the most experienced athletes. They don't just creep in during moments of doubt, they charge in at full force when the stakes are highest, often at the most inconvenient times. They appear in training, in competition and in everyday life. And, no matter how strong or seasoned you are, they never truly go away.

This isn't a sign of weakness. It's part of being human. The real question isn't if these thoughts will come, it's when and, more importantly, how you deal with them.

The mind is a powerful tool, but it's also a potential saboteur. In elite sport, where milliseconds and millimetres matter, mental clarity is everything. This is where scenario planning, psychological conditioning and pre-competition routines become critical. During a competition, the window to respond to negative thoughts is incredibly narrow. You don't have the luxury of deep reflection or lengthy self-analysis in the heat of battle. That's why preparation is key, putting procedures in place before the storm hits.

Negative thoughts aren't limited to competition either. They strike during training, during rest and often when you least expect them. Over the years, I've faced them all: doubts about myself, expectations from others, fear of failure, resentment, insecurity. I learned that these thoughts don't just go away with success; they evolve. You don't eliminate them; you develop tools to navigate through them.

Three main categories

Over time, I've come to see that negative thoughts typically fall into three major categories:

- **Thoughts about yourself**: these include self-doubt, imposter syndrome, fear of failure or results-based anxieties like, 'if I lose, I've wasted all this time'.

- **Thoughts about expectations**: the pressure of living up to past performances or external expectations, especially when others are watching or depending on you.

- **Thoughts about others**: frustrations with opponents, referees, coaches or team-mates.

Their inconvenient nature

Negative thoughts don't arrive on schedule. They appear when your guard is down, when you're tired, under pressure or facing the unknown. Sometimes they're internal:

- What if I'm not good enough?
- What happens if I lose? am I just wasting my time?

Other times, they're externalised:

- That referee's against me.
- Why do they get more support than I do?

Sometimes, they're existential:

- What am I even doing here?

The thoughts themselves aren't the problem. It's how we respond that matters.

When negative thoughts hit hard

At the Shanghai Grand Prix in 2023, I lost my first three matches in the group stage. With each defeat, the internal pressure mounted. I began to question everything: why I was there, what I was doing with my life. I even felt a physical ping in my hip. I was close to breaking point.

With only minutes before my next match, I turned to Ben, my coach, and released the flood of emotion. Speaking helped me step back from the spiral. I verbalised each irrational thought and responded to them with logic. That moment of honesty helped steady the ship. I went on to win my final pool match and reset my momentum.

By contrast, at the 2014 World Championships, I became obsessed with one thought: 'I must make day two'. The result? I fenced nervously, rushed decisions and lost 15–14. I was the only one on the team who didn't qualify. That loss taught me: when your mind is fixated on outcomes, you can't be present. And without presence, you can't perform freely.

Emotional regulation and recovery

After difficult losses, my instinct used to be isolation. I'd shut myself in a hotel room and replay the match endlessly. Over time, I learned this wasn't helpful. Instead, I adopted a better habit: write down three reflections while the emotions are fresh, then move on. It helped me release tension and keep perspective.

Michael Jordan once said: 'I've failed over and over and over again in my life. And that is why I succeed'. That idea became my anchor.

The trap of goal stacking

A common psychological trap is goal stacking, linking one goal to another in a chain of conditional success:

- If I qualify here, I can focus on the worlds.
- If I medal there, I'll be secure for Paris.

It sounds strategic, but it adds unbearable pressure. At the 2019 World Championships in Budapest, I had two coaches and a filmmaker documenting my journey. I wasn't present: I was wrapped up in expectations. I fenced poorly and lost early. The documentary never got made.

The lesson? I had outsourced responsibility for my success: onto people, events and optics. I needed to return to myself: to my own routines, my own process, my own ownership.

Scenario planning: anticipating the mind's traps

You can't have a long chat with yourself mid-bout. That's why you need scenario planning in place beforehand, anticipating emotional swings and having pre-set responses. Not affirmations, but functional tools, responses you have practised.

Between competitions or in everyday life, there's more time for deep reflection. That's when you build the resilience you'll rely on later. That's when you condition the mind, just as you condition the body.

Negative thoughts about others, especially referees

One of the most damaging distractions is fixating on referees. At the 2018 World Championships in China in a round of 32 match against Carlos Llavador, I led 12–8 before a disputed call turned the bout. I argued, I lost focus and I lost the match.

That match changed everything. Arguing breaks your rhythm and damages your performance. Referees are human; they make mistakes. But emotional reactions make things worse, not better.

I made a new rule: no more arguing. If I disagreed, I would ask respectfully and adapt. That mindset shift not only protected my focus; it made me a better fencer.

Reframing pressure before the zonal

The morning before the zonal qualifier in Luxembourg, I woke up sick. To make things more intense, my old training partner messaged me. He'd flown in from Kuwait to watch. Ten people were coming to support me. I felt the pressure mounting.

But then I reframed it: they were here for me as a person, not just an athlete. That mindset grounded me. I reminded myself of past competitions where I'd performed despite illness. And I trusted my mental preparation to carry me through.

Solutions

Here is what I learnt about managing negative thoughts:

- **Control the controllables**: you can't control the result, the referee or your opponent. But you can control your effort, your attitude and your preparation. Focus on those.

- **Contextualise and verbalise**: speak your thoughts. Whether it's with your coach, a team-mate or your journal, naming your worry helps you separate from it and respond logically.

- **Use your mental warm-up**: my pre-competition routine became a foundation. I'd rehearse emotional triggers and prepare rational counters in advance. This mental rehearsal gave me calm and focus.

- **Compartmentalise with discipline**: train your attention. When it's time to fence, fence. When it's time to rest, rest. Don't drag your stress across every area of your life. Discipline equals clarity. No matter the stresses I was facing, I knew I could focus entirely on my training session for those two hours. Whatever other concerns I had could wait until after the session and I would deal with them when the time came.

Final thoughts

You cannot live a life without negative thoughts. They will come on good days and bad, in finals and early rounds, in training and in recovery. But you can train your response.

Your mind, like your body, needs conditioning. When emotion strikes, logic must be ready. When pressure builds, presence must hold. This is the training behind the training, the work that turns potential into performance.

Whether you're chasing gold or clarity, the truth is the same: you don't control the noise, but you do control your response. In mastering that response, you unlock your power.

15

NARRATIVE BUILDING

In fencing, as in life, 90 percent of the game is mental. Athletic performance is often perceived as a physical pursuit, a matter of strength, speed or technique. But beneath the surface, where elite competitors are separated by the finest of margins, it's the mind that becomes the deciding factor. The ability to think clearly, regulate emotions and execute a plan under pressure is what ultimately determines success.

One of the most powerful psychological tools I discovered was controlling the narrative. That doesn't mean ignoring reality or pretending to be someone you're not. It means choosing the lens through which you interpret the moment. You can't always control your opponent, the referee or the conditions, but you can control the story you tell yourself before stepping into the match.

Before a big match, it's normal to feel nervous. Most athletes worry about the result, their performance or what others might think. The internal dialogue becomes consumed by fear and expectation. But shifting that inner focus outward, toward your opponent's potential weaknesses, toward a tactical mission or toward something emotionally motivating, can diffuse the pressure and create psychological space.

The science behind the story

It's about more than intuition. Sports psychologist Dr Michael Gervais, who has worked with Olympic champions and elite military units, often says: 'the story you tell yourself becomes the foundation of your performance'.

Your self-narrative affects everything from confidence to emotional regulation to decision-making under pressure. Gervais argues that elite performers create intentional narratives, stories that serve them. These are crafted, rehearsed and embedded through training and reflection. I didn't know it at the time, but I was doing just that.

One of the most powerful examples of narrative building came during a World Cup match against Gerek Meinhardt, an Olympic medallist and one of the sport's true greats. I knew that if both of us fenced our best, he would win, so I reframed the story. I told myself he was fresh but not sharp, having had a bye to the second day of fencing, while I had battled through the first day. I imagined it as a training match, stayed calm and didn't celebrate my points so as not to make Gerek move into gear and wake up. That narrative gave me the edge and I won 15–11, not because I was better, but because I believed the story I'd created.

I used the same approach against Miles Chamley-Watson at the World Championships in Wuxi. On paper, it was an impossible draw, but I leaned into the narrative of being the underdog. He was under pressure, fighting for a spot in the ultra-competitive US Olympic team, knowing he had to get a result. I framed the story as me being the hunter, the underdog with nothing to lose. I lived for these moments. It gave me the freedom to execute my plan with discipline and control. The result? Another 15–11 upset, driven not just by tactics, but by mindset.

Those two matches taught me something vital: the story you tell yourself can tip the balance: it's a lesson that I would carry forward into some of the most pivotal bouts of my Olympic campaign.

Story against Llavador

At the 2023 European Championships, I faced Carlos Llavador in the round of 32. I had never beaten Carlos before. He was a World Championship medallist and a long-time sparring partner at Frascati. In training, he often had the upper hand. But I needed something more. Something emotional. And I found it in a moment from the past.

In 2021, at the zonal qualifier for the Tokyo Olympics in Madrid, Carlos, already qualified, was commentating on me in the final match to go to the Olympics. My sister, fluent in Spanish, later told me he had made dismissive remarks about me on air. I hadn't forgotten.

That became my fuel. I locked in, listened to *Right Here, Right Now* on repeat, and got video analysis support from Raffi Rhys Pollitt. I told myself: this is payback. This is where the record changes.

I surged ahead 12–6, but Carlos adapted. He clawed back six consecutive points, bringing it to 12–12. The momentum had shifted. The moment was slipping.

But I reached for my inner story. The one where I wasn't the guy who buckled under pressure anymore. I was the guy who stood his ground. Like General Zhukov at the Battle of Stalingrad during the Second World War when he told his troops: 'not a single step back'.

I parried, riposted and scored. 13–12. Then 15–13. Victory. That day, the narrative saved me. Not just the strategy, but the belief system that backed it.

Story against Choupenitch

Not every narrative helped me. Some hurt me, especially when I didn't realise I'd built them. Alexander Choupenitch had beaten me for 13 years straight. He was my training partner, my rival for Olympic qualification and my mental kryptonite. Over the years, I built a subconscious story: you can't beat him.

Even when my fencing improved, even when I changed coaches or tactics, somewhere deep down, I didn't believe I could win. That belief became my reality.

That's the danger of the wrong narrative. It becomes a self-fulfilling prophecy. You enter the match already defeated. It's not enough to be fit, skilled, and prepared. If the story you tell yourself is that you'll fail, you probably will.

Against De Greef

Sometimes, the smallest moment can spark the biggest shift. Differdange, Luxembourg. The final Olympic qualifier. Winner goes to Paris.

Before my final bout, I passed the call room and saw Stef De Greef my opponent in the final getting physio. He looked tired with his kit off getting treatment on his leg. Whether it was real or not didn't matter, my brain locked onto it.

'He's tired. He's done. You've trained for this. This is your moment. He's ripe for the taking.'

That was all I needed. A flicker of perceived advantage to shift my belief from doubt to conviction. I entered the piste with an extra energy and a spring in my step, confident that he was more tired than me before the match had begun.

Conclusion: you are the author

In fencing, and in life, you can't always control what happens. But you can always control the story you tell yourself.

Narrative building isn't about lying to yourself. It's about choosing a perspective that fuels confidence, sharpens intent and allows you to compete from a place of strength rather than fear. When you build the right internal narrative, you create clarity.

In high-stakes environments, pressure can cloud your thinking. Fear of failure or judgment can blur your execution. But when you step into the arena with a crafted narrative when you know exactly why you're there, who you are and what you believe, you sharpen your mental game. You are the author of your own story.

16

COMPETING WITH THE BEST

On 26 April 2024, when I qualified for the Paris Olympics in Luxembourg, I shared the following message:

> Find your own path and your own style of fencing. It is, of course, important to learn from others, but if you imitate others, you will never be as good as them. Know your game well: your strengths and your weaknesses; mastering yourself is much more important than mastering your opponents. Secondly, the sport of fencing is global now and the knowledge is out there. You don't have to be from a traditional fencing nation to achieve your dreams. Finally, whether you are winning or losing, never give up.

This chapter is about that message. It's about what it truly takes to compete and win against the very best. Drawing from the training systems I was part of, the psychological methods I've explored and the tactical frameworks I built across years of elite sport, this chapter pulls together all the earlier threads: training with world-class fencers, building a narrative, sticking to mental preparation, fighting on your own terrain and delivering in the endgame.

Beating the best

Throughout my journey, I managed to defeat some of the world's top fencers who were Olympic medallists, world champions and continental giants:

- Daniele Garozzo (Italy), Olympic champion, Rio 2016
- Peter Joppich (Germany), four-time world champion
- Benjamin Kleibrink (Germany), Olympic champion, Beijing 2008
- Tomasso Marini (Italy): world champion and Olympic silver medallist, Paris 2024
- Erwan Le Pechoux (France): Olympic gold medallist, Tokyo 2020
- Alexander Cheremisinov (Russia), Olympic team champion, Rio 2016
- Ryo Miyake (Japan), Olympic silver medallist
- Miles Chamley-Watson (US): world champion
- Carlos Llavador (Spain): world bronze medallist
- Marcus Mepstead (GB): world silver medallist
- Mo Ziwei (China): Asian champion

- Taegyu Ha (South Korea): Asian champion
- Radoslow Glonek (Poland), former world number two
- Michal Siess (Poland): European Games champion

I knew I could beat anyone in the world and I was proud of that. But as my team-mate Richard Kruse once said: 'there's a difference between beating the best in the world and being the best in the world'.

Although I was incredibly proud of some of these wins, he was right. The difference was routine, delivering consistency in performance. That was the key I never quite unlocked. But on a specific day, in a specific match, with the right mental, tactical and physical preparation, I could absolutely deliver.

Fighting battles on your terrain

If you want to win, fight your battles on your own terrain, as at the Battle of Thermopylae. In 480 BC, 300 Spartans led by King Leonidas held off an invading Persian army of over 100,000. They chose to fight in a narrow mountain pass where the Persians' numerical advantage meant little. The terrain favoured discipline, skill and mental fortitude, exactly what the Spartans embodied.

This story profoundly influenced how I approached my own matches. If you try to fight the best in the world on their terms, their strengths will overwhelm you. You have to dictate the tempo, the rhythm and the style. You have to fight in a space where your game flourishes and theirs diminishes. Like Leonidas at Thermopylae, whenever I competed against stronger or more decorated opponents, I asked myself: how can I tilt the battlefield in my favour?

Fight, flight or freeze

During the semi-final of the zonal qualifier for the Paris Olympics against Jonas Winterberg Poulsen, I applied this principle in full. He was fast, powerful and aggressive, one of Europe's rising stars with a European Games silver medal to his name and the second seed at the zonal. But I'd already beaten him in the poule and I knew something important: the best way to beat a dominant attacker isn't to match their energy, it's to control the psychological tempo from the first second.

My tactic was clear: overwhelm him early. The goal was to force him into a psychological pressure cooker and trigger one of three classic stress responses:

- **Freeze**: hesitate or stall under pressure, which would allow me to land a flurry of uninterrupted hits.
- **Flight**: withdraw mentally or collapse tactically, opening the door for a scoring spree.
- **Fight**: react emotionally by abandoning his technical system, getting dragged into my kind of bout and fencing beneath his potential.

My job was to induce any of these. If I could create a storm early, pressing with speed, varied attacks and relentless intensity, Jonas would be forced to choose between instinct and execution.

I didn't give him time to think or reset. From the opening exchange, I disrupted his rhythm, pressed with precise variations and made sure the bout was fought on my terms, not his. And it worked.

He never found his flow. Whether he hesitated, panicked or fought on impulse, I stayed one step ahead by dictating the tempo and keeping him outside his comfort zone. In elite sport, it's not just about physical dominance: it's about creating the kind of psychological pressure that turns decision-makers into reactors.

When your strengths are not enough

During the Bonn World Cup in 2017 where I finished seventh, I was up against Junyuhk Kwak, a top Korean fencer. I was reminded that sometimes your strengths simply aren't enough. Before the match, my coach Ziemek Wojcieowski said: 'Koreans are faster than you. Don't try to match their footwork. Fence at your distance, at your tempo'.

That advice resonated. People often say, play to your strengths. But if your strengths are outmatched, you have to pivot. In this match, I didn't try to outrun Kwak, I outsmarted him. I changed the distance, the pace and the intensity. I made it my kind of fight.

Sometimes, your weaknesses match up better against an opponent's weaknesses than your strengths do against their strengths. The ability to adapt, tactically and psychologically, is what separates elite competitors from the rest.

The Frascati chess match

In the build-up to the 2021 European zonal qualifier for the Tokyo Olympics in Madrid, I spent several weeks training in Frascati, Italy. As borders reopened after Covid, it became one of the only training halls available to international athletes. Soon, the hall filled with the very fencers I would face for Olympic qualification: Michal Siess (world finalist), Daniel Dosa (Hungary), Martino Minuto (Turkey), Klod Yunes (Ukraine), Johannes Poscharnig (Austria) and more.

We trained together. We watched each other. Every touch was a chess move, revealing or concealing intentions. I developed a strategy. If I felt confident against someone, I avoided training with them. If I didn't, I sparred with them constantly to sharpen my tactics.

It could cause socially awkward situations. At one point, Johannes Poscharnig continued to ask me to fence and eventually I had to tell him no, as I was confident with my tactics against him. It might have given him a small mental edge, but I was playing the long game.

The endgame: holding your nerve

The hardest part of a match isn't the first touch, it's the last. Endgames are when physical fatigue peaks, adrenaline wears off and the finish line appears just close enough to make your mind wander. The scoreboard says you're almost there, but that's exactly when things get dangerous. Your focus, which carried you point by point, begins to shift. You stop thinking about what you need to do and start thinking about what might happen if you win or, worse, if you blow it.

It's when mistakes creep in, not because of lack of skill, but because of a lapse in mental discipline. I've been one point away from winning with a substantial lead and still lost. Why? Because I stopped fencing point by point. The moment I thought, I'm nearly there, I left the present moment. It was enough to break my flow, distort my decision-making and open the door for my opponent to come back.

It's as Rafael Nadal, one of the greats of tennis, says: 'play the point in front of you'. That single line encapsulates what separates good athletes from great ones. When you're up 14–11 or serving for a grand slam, the battle isn't just on the court, it's inside your head. Do you have the mental discipline to stay locked in? Can you block out the scoreboard, the crowd, the consequences?

The key is to keep focused on the process: fence the next touch with the same intensity and presence as the first. Don't fence to avoid losing. Fence to win. That means committing fully to each action, trusting your preparation and refusing to be pulled into the what-ifs of outcome-based thinking. Champions don't win by being fearless. They win by holding their nerve when it matters most. Ultimately, that is what the endgame is all about.

Final thoughts

Competing with the best goes far beyond talent or raw ability. It demands the full spectrum of performance, where the mental, tactical and emotional realms are just as vital as physical skill. It requires:

- **Tactical mastery**: knowing your game but also understanding how to break down others.

- **Psychological resilience**: the strength to endure pressure, setbacks and high-stakes moments without folding.

- **Self-awareness**: being honest about your strengths and limitations, and playing to them with intention.

- **Adaptability**: adjusting your tactics mid-bout, reading the fight and rewriting the plan if needed.

- **Unshakeable belief**: in your preparation, in your purpose and in your ability to win.

You don't need the perfect set-up, the best funding or a textbook fencing style. What you need is a vision, a strategy and the courage to fence your fight, not someone else's.

In the highest arenas of competition, the margins are razor thin. Victory doesn't always go to the most talented, but to the most prepared. The one who can hold their nerve. The one who stays present when everything is on the line.

17

HOLISTIC EFFORT

Maximum effort, what does it actually mean? In elite sport, it's easy to associate effort purely with physical training: how much you run, how hard you push, how long you stay in the gym. But maximum effort is not just physical. It is holistic. It is all encompassing.

In my sport, and in life, you cannot afford to limit your definition of hard work to one dimension. If you want to perform at your best, especially at the competition of your life, you must deliver maximum effort in every single category: physical, technical, tactical, psychological, nutritional, emotional and logistical. You cannot leave any stone unturned. Holistic effort is not just about going all in during the match, it's about going all in during every moment that leads up to it.

British Fencing: building the blueprint

My years with British Fencing's world-class performance programme laid the foundation for understanding what holistic effort really looked like. That system transformed me from a fencer into a full-time athlete. Every day, I had access to a strength and conditioning coach, a video analyst, fencing lessons, physiotherapy, a lifestyle advisor and sports psychology. I was given the full arsenal.

Despite internal politics, the support staff gave everything to help us become the best versions of ourselves. I began to understand that winning required more than talent and more than training. It required balance. It required working smart, not just hard. You needed to know your body, manage your emotions, recover properly, build tactics intelligently and align every part of your life to serve your sporting goal.

A moment of clarity in Frascati

Seven days before the qualifier for the 2021 Olympics, I was walking to the fencing hall in Frascati, Italy, just a ten-minute stroll from my apartment. Each day I would use that walk to begin my mental warm-up. But on this particular day, something was different.

Before I could start my mental warm-up I found myself smiling. I was calm and I felt something I hadn't felt in years: total clarity. I realised that, for the first time in my life, I could say with full confidence: no matter what happens, I've given it everything.

I wasn't just physically ready; I was technically sharp, tactically prepared, mentally clear and emotionally aligned. That is what holistic effort looks like. It's a type of deep personal integrity. You've done everything in your power, not just one thing. When you give everything across the board, you free yourself from regret. Whether you win or lose, you can walk away in peace.

The changing room: shared pain, shared sacrifice

After losing in the final of the European qualifier in Madrid in April 2021, one match away from reaching the Tokyo Olympics, I was broken, physically, mentally, emotionally. I had poured five years of my life into reaching that moment, only to fall short by one match. As I walked off the piste, numb, I headed to the changing room and saw Michal Siess, the Polish fencer I had beaten in the quarter-finals. We didn't speak. We didn't need to. We just looked at each other and hugged, both of us in tears.

That hug carried so much meaning. We had taken the same journey. Made the same sacrifices. Given the same holistic effort: the same early mornings, the same lonely training camps, the same exhaustion, the same physical toll, the same emotional cost. We had both done everything and yet we both had failed to reach our goal. That's why we cried, because only we knew what the other had given up to be there. That moment will stay with me forever.

Preparing for the entire journey

In the lead-up to the Olympic qualifier for Paris 2024 in Luxembourg, I planned and prepared as if I were going to win the entire tournament. That was a mindset shift.

Previously, I'd planned match by match or up to a certain point like the semi-finals. But this time, I planned every step of the journey: every match, every round, every possible scenario. My training, nutrition, strength, conditioning, emotional regulation and travel logistics were all aligned. Everything was tracked backwards from the final day of competition. That gave me control. That gave me confidence. To give myself a fighting chance I had to start by believing that I could win it. The backwards planning helped ingrain that belief inside me.

Championship behaviours

One of the most powerful external validations of this philosophy comes from Hugh McCutcheon, a coach who won Olympic gold with the US men's and women's volleyball teams. In his book *Championship Behaviours*, McCutcheon argues that excellence in sport comes from nurturing the whole person, not just the athlete. 'You can't get the best out of someone if their life is a mess. Physical excellence is built on psychological, emotional and intellectual foundations.'

He stresses that holistic development is not a luxury, it's an essential. You don't create Olympians by focusing only on their serve or footwork. You create them by cultivating resilience, structure, emotional maturity and the ability to manage pressure across the board. The best athletes in the world don't just train their legs or their lungs. They train their minds. Their habits. Their relationships. Their routines. That is what holistic effort truly is.

Final thoughts

Maximum effort is not about pushing one gear harder. It's about making sure every gear is turning. It's about giving your body, your mind, your heart and your time, all in alignment, for a single purpose.

Whether you win or lose, you can always ask: did I give everything everywhere? If the answer is yes, you walk away without regret. In the quiet moments, whether you're walking to training in Frascati or sitting on a bench in a Madrid changing room, that knowledge is more powerful than any medal.

18

LUXEMBOURG

That night, I slept like a baby and when I woke up, the day had finally arrived: 26 April 2024 in Differdange, Luxembourg. I did my breathing and mental warm-up exercises, packed my bag and headed down to breakfast. There were no fencers or coaches in sight, which meant no small talk or awkward conversations. I could enjoy my breakfast in peace.

Towards the end of the Olympic cycle, I had started booking unofficial hotels where fewer fencers would stay. It wasn't because I disliked fencers: far from it, I liked them. But I'm a talker and, if I stayed in those official hotels, I'd end up chatting endlessly and wasting precious energy. Secondly, when you stay in the same hotel as everyone else, you can't escape. Every corner you turn, every lift you step into, there's a fencer. I preferred having some downtime and detachment from that world before the competition. I would see enough of them on the piste.

So, my coach, my physio and I set off from the hotel, and our analyst for the day was ready to join us online. This was a team I had carefully built, people I trusted, experts in their fields, and who understood me, knew what worked best for me and were professional enough to push me toward peak performance.

Maria Goriup had been working with Team GB as a physiotherapist since 2014, initially with British Fencing and also with other Olympic sports like badminton. She had experience with world-class set-ups, was highly professional and fully bought into our mission. Not only did she provide treatment, but she also designed and monitored my strength and conditioning programme. Maria knew all my pre-existing injuries and how to manage them, ensuring I was physically ready.

Raffi Rhys Pollit, the man behind the scenes, was integral to the video analysis and psychological profiling of my opponents. This aspect of preparation had become essential to my performance. Without Raffi, it would have been impossible to be so well prepared. Since September, we had been working on analysing every potential opponent for this day. Raffi had watched over 30 hours of fencing footage. His work was invaluable.

Then there was Ben Peggs, my coach. Two years ago, when deciding who to work with, I remembered how well we'd collaborated back in 2017 when I came seventh at the Bonn World Cup in Germany. Ben had known me since I was 13 and we had trained together for years. He understood my fencing style deeply and he was a solid technical coach. However, Ben had a lot of responsibilities with other fencers and multiple coaching roles. Therefore, we had streamlined our collaboration. I took responsibility for season planning, preparation and a lot of the work leading up to the competition. Ben could focus on when I really needed him and our teamwork was harmonious. I would share feedback from my training sessions, and we would refine and hone everything in our lessons together. I switched to Ben to be prepared for this exact day, knowing I could count on him when the stakes were highest.

Fencing may be an individual sport, but success doesn't happen in isolation. Some fencers are lucky enough to be part of larger national programmes with full support systems. But even if you're not, it's essential to build your team around you. This includes not only those at the competition, your coach, physio and analyst, but also the emotional support of family and friends. It truly takes a village to achieve success in anything you do.

Arriving at the venue

We arrived at the venue and one of the first things we needed to do was find a place to leave our gear for the day. Maria, thanks to the reconnaissance she did the day before, found a secluded changing room away from the main fencing hall. It may seem like a small detail, but it was a huge win. Having a quiet, private space meant we could retreat and relax between matches, away from the intense energy of other competitors. Even if you're not fencing, just being in the main hall can expose you to the nerves, tension and stress of others. Being removed from that allowed us to stay calm and focused. It was a masterstroke in controlling our environment.

The game plan

We had meticulously planned out the schedule for the day, down to the minute, all the way to the gold medal match. Even if we didn't achieve the ultimate goal, we knew the execution of our plan was solid. The structure of the day would follow this sequence:

- **Mental warm-up**: breathing exercises, visualisation and mentally preparing for different scenarios.
- **Physical warm-up**: active stretching and dynamic movements.
- **Technical warm-up**: fencing lesson and sparring.
- **Competition preparation**: transport kit to the piste, fence and then repeat.
- **Post-match recovery**: recovery shake, treatment from Maria, rest.

This plan was in line with controlling the controllables. Of course, the day wouldn't go 100 percent according to plan, but if we managed to stick to it 90 percent of the time, we would be in an excellent position for each match.

Group stage strategy

There were 25 fencers from 25 countries and I was seeded sixth in the competition. The group stage had four pools of six fencers and Carlos Llavador, the number one seed, had a bye, which meant he would skip the group stage and go straight to the knock-out round.

The strategy for the group stage was clear: win all six matches, which give me a higher seeding, a likely bye through the round of 32 and a direct start in the round of 16. It would also mean avoiding Carlos Llavador until the final, where, with the pressure on him as the favourite, anything could happen.

Execution of the plan

I arrived at my piste at 08:45, 15 minutes before the start of the competition. My friends, family and coaching staff were there. By 9am, it was time to fence and get into the zone. The key to success was clear: focus on each match one at a time, not the overall outcome. I knew that to achieve the desired result of avoiding Llavador, I needed to give everything in my preparation, mentally, physically and technically.

The group stage went incredibly well. In my head, I was fencing one point at a time, keeping my mind on the process, not the results. Before each match, Ben and I ran over the specific tactics for my opponent and I was fully locked in to execute. By the end of the group stage, I had won all six matches, finishing with a victory rate of 100 percent. It meant I would be seeded second for the elimination rounds, securing a bye through the round of 32 and starting directly in the round of 16.

After thanking my friends and family for their support, I headed back to our secluded changing room. Following the plan, I took my recovery shake, received treatment from Maria, changed into fresh clothes and ate some food. I put on my headphones to decompress and listen to music, enjoying the calm away from the hustle and bustle of the competition hall. This break between rounds was a vital part of staying fresh and focused for the next challenge.

Round of 16 against Remi Brunner

In the round of 16, my opponent was Remi Brunner of Switzerland. My long-time friend, training partner and teammate Chris Nagle had come to support me. He was in charge of watching Brunner's earlier matches live and feeding back any relevant information to my coach, Ben, to determine if we needed to tweak our plan.

I was a bit nervous about Brunner, mostly due to our last encounter. During a training camp in Belgium over Christmas 2023, we had fenced each other in a team event. My team was leading 40–36, but in the final match, Brunner overcame me and we lost 45–43. That loss lingered in my mind, as I couldn't quite figure out his timing and actions during the camp.

Raffi and I had gone over the video analysis of Brunner and it was clear that while his defence was solid, his attack was much weaker. We decided to adapt my game plan by focusing on my defence and letting Brunner make mistakes while attacking, rather than clashing strengths by pitting my attack against his defence. I would have to be more patient, take my time and fence more from defence than usual.

The match started off slowly and my nerves were evident with the score tied at 3–3. But as I began to relax, I executed the pre-planned tactics more effectively, took my time and slowly gained control of the bout. It was a slow burner, but eventually, I found my rhythm and secured a comfortable win. I was through to the quarter-finals.

Quarter-final against Luka Gaganidze

Following the match, I stuck to my recovery routine, including taking my recovery shake and receiving treatment from Maria. Chris Nagle went to watch the outcome of the next match between Kristjian Archer (GB) and Luka Gaganidze (Georgia) to see who my quarter-final opponent would be.

Both Archer and Gaganidze were aggressive fencers who would come out strong from the start. In truth, I wanted to face Kristjian

Archer. He's a good friend, but I hadn't forgotten his comments about my weight. Now that I had lost seven kilos and was in prime physical condition, I was ready to prove a point. Symbolically, I put on the same tight blue top that I had worn in Mexico when I received those comments. It fitted perfectly this time and I felt ready for battle.

In the end, Gaganidze defeated Archer 15–14 and I would face him for a place in the semi-finals. I had a 100 percent win record against Gaganidze, including knocking him out at the same stage in the previous Olympic qualifier in Madrid in 2021. He was a strong, physical fencer who often thrived against technically superior or higher ranked opponents because they tended to underestimate him. But I wasn't going to make that mistake.

I had a clear game plan: I would attack, win the middle ground and keep the intensity high. With the score close at 8–6 in my favour, Gaganidze couldn't keep up with my relentless pace and pressure. I pulled ahead and won comfortably 15–8. I was now into the semi-finals, one match away from the final and a ticket to Paris 2024.

A shift in fortune: Llavador's unexpected defeat

As I shook hands with my opponent, his coach and the referees, while thanking my support team, something caught my eye. A sizable crowd had gathered around piste 2 at the far end of the hall. This usually happened when a match became interesting or intense as it approached its final moments. The match in question was between Petar Files of Croatia and the tournament favourite, Carlos Llavador of Spain.

Files was a strong, athletic and tall fencer who had already knocked out one of the favourites, Klod Yunes, in the previous round. As I glanced over, I saw the score was tied 10–10 during their one-minute break at the end of the first round. A memory of a mistake from three years ago flashed in my mind, when Poscharnig was leading Choupenitch 11–7 and I had stayed to watch, only for the result to flip. I decided not to linger this time. Whatever would be, would be.

I headed back to our secluded changing room with a break of 2½ hours before the semi-final. I followed my usual recovery protocols, then sat down to rest, listening to music. About ten minutes later, my friend Chris Nagle walked into the changing room. We exchanged no words but locked eyes. Then, in perfect unison, we both burst into shocked laughter, followed by a gasp from me. He didn't need to say anything. I knew exactly what had happened. Llavador had lost.

It was a massive turn-up, a psychological boost for me. The bit of luck that hadn't fallen my way in the previous Olympic qualifier had now landed perfectly. Carlos Llavador was a world-class fencer, unlucky not to qualify directly off the ranking. It's true that I believed I could beat anyone. I had defeated Carlos just last season and I had a plan for our potential bout, but the reality was that if we both fenced our best, he would likely win.

I allowed myself a brief moment of indulgence, savouring the news. It's a normal reaction when the unexpected happens. But after a minute or two, I knew I had to return my focus to the process. I couldn't let this sudden shift in fortune throw off my mental preparation.

Now, a few thoughts crossed my mind. This was my year. It was my moment. The remaining three fencers, while strong and ranked higher than me on paper, didn't have my level of experience nor were they as battle hardened. I knew what it took to perform under pressure in competitions like this. With that boost in my mindset, I returned to my process and the schedule we had carefully laid out.

Semi-final showdown: preparation and mental fortitude

We were now moving to a different hall for the semi-final match, which would take place 2½ hours later. This longer break gave me plenty of time to recover, refuel and prepare for the upcoming bout. Unlike three years ago, where the final followed just ten minutes after the second semi-final, I now had a 1¼ hour gap between the semi-final and the final, if I were to win. This change was critical, giving me more time to rest and be ready for the final push.

During the extended rest period, I focused on conserving as much energy as possible. I stayed in the changing room the entire time, avoiding conversations with other fencers or even my cheer squad. Detachment was key here. I wanted to relax and preserve both mental and physical energy, ensuring that I didn't cramp like I had three years ago.

Time crept up quickly. Soon I was ready to take a lesson with Ben before we moved to the final hall, which was in a different location. However, we decided to do the lesson once we arrived at the call room. The call room is where fencers wait before their matches, especially toward the later stages of the competition, like semi-finals and finals. Here, equipment is checked and the idea is to ensure everything runs on schedule.

Arriving with 40 minutes before the start of the semi-final, I began my warm-up routine, grabbing my sword and mask to take a quick lesson with Ben. But then, things took a sudden turn for the worse. A member of the call-room staff decided to go on a power trip, telling us we weren't allowed to warm up or take a lesson outside the call room. It was ridiculous. Athletes should absolutely be entitled to warm up, especially 40 minutes before the match. We weren't even obliged to be in the call room until 20 to 30 minutes before the match and I was using training equipment, not my competition gear.

Unfortunately, this is where Ben and I have different philosophies. When I was balancing university studies with my fencing career, I always prioritised fencing over attending lectures. I once asked if I could skip a lecture and catch up later, but the request was denied. A lifestyle coach from British Fencing once gave me advice that stuck with me: 'it's better to seek forgiveness than ask for permission'. Ben, however, is the opposite, more cautious. He became nervous, telling me, 'Alex, you're going to get disqualified'. I was certain it wasn't going to happen. I just needed five minutes to run through the techniques and tactics for the next match.

We completed the lesson and, with 30 minutes to spare, I entered the call room. Ben was still worried about a disqualification, but I didn't have the headspace to deal with his anxiety. Luckily, Maria, my physio, stepped in. I quickly explained the situation and she helped calm Ben down.

As I sat in the call room, the same official who had disrupted my warm-up preparation continued to annoy me. She told me to take off my headphones, despite others wearing theirs. I handed over my headphones and sat there, trying to stay focused. She even continued giving me verbal jabs as we waited for the presentation before the semi-final.

But here's the thing: in my head, this was my moment. I had been preparing for this for three years, mentally and physically. Over time, I had trained for different scenarios to knock me off balance: schedule delays, referee mistakes and more. In my 21-year career, I had dealt with countless obstacles, jet lag, insomnia, death, injustice, losing my fencing bag at the airport. This wasn't going to derail me. I let her words go in one ear and out the other, refocusing on the task at hand: my opponent, Jonas Winterburg Poulsen of Denmark.

Tactical precision against Jonas Winterburg Poulsen

At 21, Jonas was one of Europe's rising stars. He had recently won an individual silver medal at the European Games in Poland and was the second highest ranked fencer in the competition. As the official continued her dressing-down, I noticed Jonas had his psychologist with him. He observed the situation with a semi-smirk, possibly thinking it was less than ideal preparation for me. What he didn't know was how much mental work I had done to deal with scenarios like this, training myself to shift from emotional-based thinking to rational, process-driven thinking.

I knew exactly what tactics to execute. I had fenced Jonas earlier that day in the poule and won, which validated my tactics. I also observed him closely, watching his facial expressions, body language and stance. There's much to learn from your opponent before the match even begins.

Jonas exuded confidence, and I got the sense he believed if he stuck to his game, he would win. But my plan was to make sure he couldn't play his game. Based on the video analysis we had done with Raffi, we knew Jonas liked to pressure his opponents and pick them off with attacks. My tactic was to put pressure on him with explosive attacks right from the start, overwhelming him psychologically and technically. If he adapted, I would slightly modify my attacks, adjusting the finish or timing.

It was a key difference from three years ago. If my plan A didn't work, I wouldn't switch to plan B (defence). My plan B was now an adaptation of plan A. For instance, if my step-lunge wasn't working, I could change the timing or feint to create openings. Richard Kruse had once said to me: 'it is one move done a thousand different ways or a thousand moves done one way'. This was about adapting within my strengths, not abandoning them.

Putting pressure on Jonas from the outset was not just about scoring points, it was psychological warfare. I had been fencing for ten more years than him, and I knew what it felt like when your opponent comes out with an unexpected style and intensity. It's disorienting. When faced with such pressure, opponents often choose between fight or flight. If they choose flight, they become paralysed and you can rack up points. If they fight, they abandon their technical game, which can also work in your favour if you're the better fencer. I had practised this strategy for hours every day with Raffi, so I was prepared either way.

The semi-final: executing the plan

The hall for the finals was packed with about 150 spectators and I could see my supporters in the crowd. They made up about 10 percent of the audience and I realised their presence wasn't adding pressure, it was energising me. I was a born performer, ready to put on a show. As we saluted and I high-fived Ben, I felt ready. The match started explosively. I scored four points within the first nine seconds, catching Jonas completely off guard. He was in flight mode, visibly frustrated as it wasn't the start he had expected.

We traded points and Jonas gradually got into the match. He finally took the lead at 8–7, the first time in the entire tournament I was behind. A moment of doubt crept in, but that's why I had chosen Ben to be my coach. I turned to him and his calm trigger words helped me refocus.

I adapted my tactics slightly, just enough to throw Jonas off again and regained control. I took an 11–8 lead and we traded points until the score was 13–12 in my favour. Ben's trigger words kept me locked in and I scored the next two touches to win 15–12.

Cool, calm and collected, I didn't celebrate loudly. I knew there was still a job to do. I allowed myself a small fist pump, grabbed my swords and glanced at the crowd. Seeing my supporters, I couldn't resist shouting, 'come on!'. In response, I heard cheers and shouts from my friends and family.

Looking back on this match, it showcased my growth as a fencer. I had won 15–12 in just 57 seconds, fencing with intense pressure and aggression, yet it was a controlled, thoughtful performance. It was a stark contrast to when I won the British Championship in 2013, which was an ultra-defensive battle that went into overtime at 0–0. This victory in the semi-final highlighted how much I had developed, both mentally and tactically. I was now able to access my mental skills consistently, pre-programming my mind with tactics and scenario training, and, crucially, I had developed the adaptability needed to tweak my plans in the heat of battle. One match now stood between me and my Olympic dream.

This was it, three years after the loss in the final of the European Olympic qualifier in Madrid, I was back again, one match away from realising my lifelong dream: qualifying for the Olympic Games.

Presence in the final

I had 1¼ hour to prepare for the biggest moment of my life. Surprisingly, I wasn't thinking about the Olympics or what it meant. Instead, I was laser-focused on the process, living fully in the present. My day had been meticulously planned, minute by minute, so I stuck to the plan and recovery protocols. I took my recovery shakes, got stretched down by Maria, changed my clothes and rested.

Standing between me and the Olympics was Stef De Greef from Belgium. He was a tall, left-handed fencer, ranked number three going into the competition. Initially, Raffi and I had expected a different Belgian fencer, Stef Van Campenhout, to compete at the zonal. However, De Greef had overtaken his compatriot after an impressive eighth place at the Washington Grand Prix a month earlier. Because of this last-minute switch, De Greef was the most recent opponent Raffi and I had analysed, making him fresh in my mind.

De Greef was a top contender. I'd heard people mention his name frequently when talking about potential winners of the zonal. However, his slow, rhythmic style of fencing matched up well with my own tactics. His strength was in controlling the pace, picking off mistakes and using his height advantage. For me, the key was not to play on his terrain. Raffi and I had discussed that if I took it to him with high intensity and explosivity, forcing him to fight on my terms, I'd have the advantage. I had to pull him out of his comfort zone.

I also reminded myself of something I'd been repeating throughout the Olympic cycle: I was an experienced, world-class fencer. I was 31, seven years older than Stef, and I had a lot more experience, including a previous final at this competition. I knew what to expect, while for Stef, it was his first time in such a high-stakes scenario.

About 35 minutes before the match, as I passed the call room, I saw De Greef getting physio treatment, looking sweaty and fatigued. Whether he was actually tired or not didn't matter; to me, it was a sign, a flashback to how I had felt three years ago in a similar situation.

Seeing him like that gave me energy. I told myself, he's tired. He's ready to be taken down.

When it was time, we were called to the finals' piste. I fist-pumped Ben, saluted the fans and stepped up to face the final battle. Everything was on the line. After 21 years of hard work and sacrifice, highs and lows, it all came down to this moment. But honestly, my focus was on the present, on executing the first touch with the trigger phrase in my mind: small first step.

The referee called us to *en garde* and we tested our weapons. The match began with the call to fence and I came flying out of the blocks. Within four seconds, I had scored three points. I was already up 3–0.

After that first touch, I felt a bit of cramp in my leg and for a split second thought, 'oh no, not again, not like last time'. But I remembered Maria's advice: sometimes cramps come from nerves, not dehydration or lack of fitness. I shook out my legs, reminded myself that I was fit and hydrated, and the feeling disappeared. I reset my focus.

Stef was clearly startled by my explosive start. He wasn't expecting this pace, especially since he had been fencing at a slower, more controlled rhythm all day. I built my lead to 8–4 and then to 11–8. Each time I conceded a hit, I quickly refocused and stuck to my plan, taking it one point at a time.

At 13–8, I scored two quick points and found myself just two touches away from the Olympics. For the first time in the match, my mind briefly wandered to the result. I thought, 'oh my God, you're going to the Olympics'. But I had prepared for this moment of result-based thinking. I immediately pulled myself back into the present, repeating my trigger phrase: small first step. I scored another point: 14–8. No time to waste. I got back *en garde*, ready for the final point.

I lunged and scored the 15th touch, a fast attack. I can't explain how many times I had dreamt of this moment. I had visualised every part of it, taking off my mask, looking up to the sky imagining my father smiling down at me, shaking hands with my opponent and then calling my mother onto the piste for a big hug, telling her, 'we did it. We're going to the Olympics'.

When I scored that 15th touch, I couldn't believe it was over. I stood there, still ready for the next point, unable to comprehend that my lifelong dream had just come true. It felt like there should be another hurdle, another match, but there wasn't. It was done. I was going to the Olympics.

After shaking hands with Stef, my mother and physio Maria ran onto the piste, cheering. I then embraced my coach Ben in a big hug, while everyone who had supported me started to gather around. In the meantime, my mother had run off to retrieve a massive Cypriot flag that was hanging in the finals' hall. After hugging Ben, I turned around, shouting, 'mum!'. She handed the flag to my friend Chris and I gave her a huge hug, whispering in her ear, 'we did it! I told you we would do it'. It was an incredible moment. My mother, who had signed me up for fencing lessons at age seven, now, at 31, I was embracing her after booking my ticket to the Paris Olympics 2024.

There was a women's final due to start, but, honestly, we were going to have our moment. I called everyone who had travelled to support me up onto the raised piste. Their support over the years, particularly on that day, had helped me achieve my lifelong goal. Positivity breeds positivity and they had created a special environment of encouragement and belief.

The feeling was as much a sense of relief as it was elation. Many people came up to congratulate me, but it was all a blur. I think I had reached my maximum dopamine level. I didn't even have time or mental capacity to process what had just happened. After changing out of my gear, I joined those who had supported me for a small beer to toast the moment.

We had about 30 minutes to wait while the women's final took place, but I was completely spent, mentally, physically and emotionally. After the match had finished, I was presented with a cardboard ticket that read, 'Ticket to Paris 2024'. I had finally achieved my lifelong dream after 24 years of fencing. After the heartbreak of missing out on London, Rio and Tokyo, I had found my redemption. I would be competing in Paris.

Moreover, I had made history. As a fencer from the small island of Cyprus, I became its first-ever fencer to qualify for the Olympic Games, a proud moment not just for me but for my country.

At the time, none of it really sank in. Ben, Maria and I took a taxi back to the hotel, utterly exhausted. Chris Nagle and my mother were busy organising the evening's celebrations. We managed to shower and muster enough energy to immortalise the day in the memory of all those who had been on the journey with me.

We arrived at the restaurant around 9pm. Dinner flowed with drinks and I gave a series of rambling speeches, going through each person in attendance and sharing anecdotes, explaining just how much I appreciated them being there and everything they had done for me.

I paused for a moment, looking around the table. I felt so humbled. So many people had come to support me, making great personal sacrifices. They had been there for me through thick and thin, during the highs and the lows. For me, this victory wasn't just mine; it was theirs as well. All I can say is that it was a truly memorable night and the occasion was celebrated as it deserved to be.

The next day, we travelled back to London. Both of my phones were buzzing non-stop with messages of support from Cyprus, Britain and all over the world. As I read through the messages, I became emotional, realising how many people cared about me and had been cheering for me to succeed.

It still didn't feel real and I wondered when it would finally sink in. The reality was that I had meticulously planned everything up until the day of the zonal championships on 26 April. But beyond that? Nothing. At that moment, I was just satisfied with achieving my lifelong dream of qualifying for the Olympic Games. I hadn't yet thought about what came next. Of course, I believed I could do it, but I hadn't planned much beyond that victorious moment.

CONCLUSION: PARIS

True to form, I wasn't able to take things one step at a time. A week after qualifying for the Olympics, I decided to start the next chapter of my life by proposing to my then-girlfriend Sarah at Hyde Park. I was so confident in my compartmentalisation skills that I thought, 'Olympic Games, marriage, moving out, no problem. What could go wrong?'

Mentally, however, it became more of a struggle than expected. I knew I was capable of beating anyone on the day. I had proved that in Luxembourg. But I wasn't sure if I had the mental fortitude to do it again, twice in three months. After all, I had finally achieved a lifetime goal of qualifying for the Olympic Games after 20 years of hard work and sacrifice.

The difficulty lay in shifting my focus. For so long, my dream was to qualify for the Olympics. Now I was going, it was tough to reignite the drive to perform at my best at the Games. If I'm being honest, my goal had evolved over the years. When I was 16, I would have said my ambition was to become an Olympic champion. That was the ultimate prize for any athlete, the undisputed title of being the best in the world. But as the years went by, and with each Olympic cycle I missed, my subconscious goal seemed to shift. My ego craved the recognition and gratification of simply qualifying for the Olympics.

So, even though I was thrilled to be heading to Paris, I had to fight the temptation to rest on my laurels and be satisfied with merely qualifying. I needed to shift my mindset toward competing well and giving my best performance, regardless of the outcome.

One mental safety net, however, was that my family, friends and all of Cyprus were proud of me just for qualifying. The messages of support I received after securing my spot were overwhelming As one of only 15 athletes to qualify for the Cyprus Olympic team and the first fencer in the history of the island to do so, I wanted to leave the Olympics knowing I had done everything within my power to perform at my best and have no regrets.

Balancing life's milestones

In addition to the Olympic preparation, I had another major life event unfolding: my partner and I had decided to get married on 18 August, just under three weeks after my competition in Paris. It meant I had a lot to juggle in a short period of time: preparing for the Olympics, planning my wedding, moving out of my house and running my business, Inspion Sports.

It wasn't just about preparing as an athlete. I was my own coach, psychologist, team manager and logistics coordinator, responsible for planning my team's travel and organising their accommodation. Beyond that, the Olympics represented a rare window for exposure

CONCLUSION

in the world of fencing: a sport that only really shines during this three-week period every four years. This was my chance to leverage that exposure for sponsorships, future career prospects and personal growth beyond fencing.

It was an incredibly demanding task to balance all these responsibilities, but luckily, I had a great support network. My family, friends, team-mates and colleagues helped me manage the pressure and reminded me that, despite the challenges, I was on the verge of achieving something truly remarkable.

The skill of compartmentalisation became invaluable during this time. I dedicated each part of my day to a specific aspect of my life, whether it was training, work or personal matters. If certain tasks could be delegated, I entrusted them to others and I always started my day with a mental warm-up. Before training, my mind would often be crowded with thoughts and concerns from different areas of my life, but by the end of my mental warm-up, I was ready to focus on fencing.

The key was applying logic to my emotional concerns. I reminded myself that the time I was spending training, whether for two or three hours, was strictly for fencing. Worrying about other matters during training wouldn't change anything, so I reset myself on my specific training goals. This approach cleared my head and prepared me mentally for the task at hand.

However, there were still moments when intrusive thoughts would pop up while I was working on something else. In those instances, I first acknowledged the thought, applied logic to it and, if that didn't calm my emotional side, I turned to my breathing exercises. I would breathe in deeply, pushing out my stomach, hold my breath and then exhale through my mouth, refocusing on the breath each time another thought surfaced. This technique, which I had practised many times, allowed me to regain control and stay on course.

For the past eight years representing Cyprus, I had worn many hats as athlete, coach, psychologist and logistics manager. When I was part of Team GB, everything was done for me. My training was planned, coaches provided and travel logistics taken care of.

With Cyprus, my system worked for the most part, but for major multi-sport events like the Olympics, I also had to navigate the rules of the International Olympic Committee and the Cyprus Olympic Committee. Fortunately, everything came together in time, and my support staff received their accreditations. Although Raffi and Maria had only temporary accreditations for day visits, it was enough. With that settled, I could finalise my plans for Paris.

For my supporters, my sister took charge of organising the logistics for around twelve of them to come and watch me. In addition to them, there were others who would be there on their own. Regardless of the outcome, I knew that I would be surrounded by those who mattered most and that we would be able to celebrate the journey together afterward.

Arrival and settling in

On 23 July, Maria, Raffi and I were set to meet for our journey to the Olympics. I spent the day before meticulously packing, ensuring everything was ready for the trip. My Cyprus Olympic kit would be waiting for me at the village. That morning, my mum and I took a bus to King's Cross, which was supposed to be a 20-minute journey but turned into a 40-minute ordeal. To make matters worse, the bus driver stopped to 'regulate the service', so we jumped off and grabbed

CONCLUSION

an Uber. However, the driver refused to take my fencing bag, claiming it was too big. My mum and I half-walked, half-ran, arguing along the way about whose fault it was that we might miss the train to the Olympics.

We arrived at King's Cross, sweating, with an hour to spare. I went through security and met Raffi and Maria, who were already waiting. Seeing the sweat on my forehead, they laughed and said, 'typical Tofalides!'.

During our journey, I noticed spectators wearing Team GB or Paris 2024 shirts, excited to attend the Games. Despite being an Olympian, I had always felt a bit uncomfortable talking about my fencing achievements. There was a sense of imposter syndrome that came with it, especially since fencing is a niche sport and few can make a living from it. However, fencing demands great physical, technical and psychological skill. I had earned my place at the Olympics and decided then to fully embrace the experience. We arrived at Paris Gare du Nord, where a gentleman holding an Olympics sign ushered us into a minibus heading to the Olympic Village.

It was a place like no other. Each country had its own living quarters with flags draped over the buildings. It felt like a bubble, where people from every corner of the world coexisted, focused on sport, friendship and peace, while the world's problems stayed outside.

The first place we visited was the dining hall, which had cuisines from around the world. The food itself wasn't remarkable, but the people-watching was. You could spot athletes from various sports and countries and try to guess their sport based on their physique. Raffi and I even managed to chat with some North Korean athletes and exchange pins, a common activity in the Olympic Village.

Exploring the village, we discovered a gym, a hairdresser, a relaxation room and I picked up my free Samsung phone. With so much going on, it was easy to get swept up in the excitement and forget we were there to compete.

We arrived on Wednesday, 24 July, and my competition would be on Monday, 29 July. Over the years, I'd come to prefer arriving closer to competition day to avoid my mind wandering or losing sight of why I was there. Since there was no jet lag to worry about, I had enough time to acclimatise, enjoy the experience and focus on getting ready for my event.

We set a training schedule: fencing in the mornings, then physio treatment and video analysis in the afternoons on Thursday, Friday, and Saturday. The opening ceremony was on Friday and, by then, we had already acclimatised to the village. Despite the distractions, we struck a great balance between soaking in the Olympic atmosphere and staying focused on the competition.

One of the things I loved most about multi-sport events was meeting athletes from different sports and countries. The rules of our sports may differ, but the dedication and application to our respective journeys were the same. I've always believed you can learn something from anyone and this environment offered endless opportunities for inspiration.

The opening ceremony

The Paris Olympics had a unique and unforgettable opening ceremony. It embraced the beauty of the city by moving away from the traditional stadium setting and taking place along the River Seine.

CONCLUSION

Each participating nation was paraded by boat, offering a stunning view of iconic landmarks like the Eiffel Tower.

I knew that despite my focus on performance, it was a once-in-a-lifetime experience I couldn't miss. The Cypriot team had a special uniform for the occasion, an olive-green jacket and white trousers, Ben, my coach, was especially elated. We had known each other since we were 13. but accreditation had put his attendance in doubt.

We joined the rest of the Cypriot delegation at the Olympic Village, ready to board buses that would take us to the boats lined up on the Seine. It was magical seeing every country walking in their traditional outfits. We found ourselves next to the Mongolian delegation.

As we waited to board, rain began to fall. The weather had been sunny and 30°C for the past few days so, of course, it had to rain on the day of the ceremony. Volunteers handed out ponchos, which offered temporary respite. We boarded the boat alongside the delegations from Colombia and Comoros and, by some stroke of luck, we were positioned right at the front.

The rain had lightened by the time we set off and we began our 30-minute sail along the Seine. The experience was surreal. We waved at other countries' boats as we passed by and, as we neared the heart of Paris, crowds lined the banks of the river, cheering loudly.

Throughout the journey, I noticed random performances, a cellist atop a building here, a guitarist playing a tune there, adding to the magic of the experience. The ceremony was taking place over several hours with grand performances occurring all around us.

Then the heavens opened again. Torrential rain poured down and I faced a dilemma: do I stay dry under my poncho or brave the rain for the sake of representing Cyprus in my official uniform? I chose the latter. Getting soaked added to the charm of the moment. I wanted my clear ten seconds of fame on live TV, not hidden under a poncho.

My sister messaged to let me know that Cyprus's moment on TV would be soon. As luck would have it, the broadcast cut to a different part of the ceremony and we spent another 20 minutes in the rain. Finally, the warning came from the organisers that we were next.

We passed under a bridge and the camera panned to us. In that moment, I waved, smiled and proudly represented my family, my country and everything I had worked for. Despite being soaked, it was one of the most magical moments of my life. Ben and I exchanged a look. He said, 'finally, we made it to the Olympic Games'.

Afterward, we managed to take some amazing photos with the Eiffel Tower in the background. The boat docked and we had the option to head to Trocadéro for the after-party or return to the Olympic Village. I chose to return to the Village, enjoying the experience, but keeping my focus on the competition ahead.

Final preparations

Saturday was the last day of training and I took a short lesson to fine-tune my game. I felt ready. That was when the draw was confirmed. I would face Adrian Wojtowiak of Poland in the round of 64. If I won, I would face the world number two, Nick Itkin. We had, of course, prepared for both opponents, but the focus for now was on Wojtowiak.

When thinking about my opponents, I often reflect on their psychology as well. It helps settle my own nerves. I considered the pressure Wojtowiak must have been feeling. Although ranked fifth in the world, Poland had opted to select its Olympic team based on national rankings. As a result, Lesek Rajski, who was ranked higher internationally, was left off the team, causing controversy in Poland. I knew Wojtowiak was under immense pressure to prove himself. In addition, I had comfortably beaten him last season. Given the choice between fencing me or Kruz Schembri, a 17-year-old fencer from the Virgin Islands, I was sure he would have preferred the latter.

That afternoon, something interesting happened outside the athletes' dining hall. We bumped into the Polish fencing team, many of whom Ben and I knew well from training camps over the years. I shook hands with Michal Siess and then Wojtowiak. He couldn't meet my eyes during the handshake and my inner emotional chimp thought I had already won the match.

I've always believed in showing no fear to my opponents and maintaining eye contact. I remembered a match in Shanghai against Daiki Fujino of Japan. The score was close and, after a break, Fujino stared into my eyes before putting his mask on. It felt like he was trying to break me psychologically, but I stared right back, refusing to look away. I won the match 15–12 and afterward, Simon Sun, a friend of Chris Nagle's, gifted me a piece of jade, saying, 'I know you're a warrior now. That stare was your way of saying, I'm ready for battle'.

Meeting the president

Sunday, the day before my competition, was a rest day. The Cyprus Olympic Committee informed us that the president of the republic, Nikos Christodoulides, would be visiting the Olympic Village. It wasn't something I usually involved myself in, as it wasn't directly related to performance. But, as my mother reminded me, who can say no to the president? So, I brought my sword and mask, just in case.

When the president arrived, we were introduced one by one. He wished me luck and, with Raffi ready with his camera, I asked if we could take a photo with the swords. It turned into an impromptu fencing lesson for the president and we got some fantastic shots of the experience. Afterward, we thanked everyone and went to lunch.

I returned to my room while Ben, Maria and Raffi explored the Village. Up until this point, I had truly enjoyed the Olympic experience and everything had been stress free.

Pre-match anxiety

However, on Sunday evening, 28 July, less than 16 hours before my first match, I started to feel the weight of the competition. Questions flooded my mind: what if I let the president down? what if I let down my family, friends and all the people back home who had supported me? Messages of encouragement from Cyprus were pouring in on social media, but instead of reassurance, they made me fear failure more. The thought of losing the first match, after all the sacrifices people had made to support me, felt crushing.

I had to call upon every mental skill I had developed over the years. I worked hard to apply rational, logical thinking to my emotional doubts. I reminded myself of all the preparation I had done, physically, mentally and technically. I had a plan not just for the match but for the entire day. My team was there to support me. If I followed my plan and gave it my all, I would be content with the outcome, knowing there was nothing more I could have done. It was a moment to trust the process and focus on giving my best effort.

We got the bus schedule and it was going to be an early wake-up: 5:30am with my match scheduled to start at 9:25am. That night, I couldn't sleep. In the past eight years at over 70 competitions, I'd never had trouble falling asleep before a match. Of course, Ben, with whom I was sharing the room, was out cold and snoring after five minutes.

Luckily, I knew from past experiences with insomnia before competitions that sleep wouldn't affect my performance. I probably slept lightly for about four to five hours. Before I knew it, the alarm went off. We showered, grabbed our bags and rushed to the canteen for a quick breakfast before bundling onto the bus to the venue. During the journey, I did my mental warm-up and breathing exercises as we headed to the Grand Palais.

It's the most remarkable venue in which to fence. Originally constructed for the Exposition Universelle in 1900, the Grand Palais is an iconic architectural masterpiece, known for its enormous glass-domed roof and intricate ironwork, symbolising the grandeur and elegance of the Belle Époque. Over the years, it's hosted numerous cultural, artistic and sporting events. For fencing, it could hold up to 9,000 spectators each day. When we arrived early that morning, it was still pretty empty, so I took a moment to admire the venue, the pistes and the sheer grandeur of it all. I couldn't believe that the Cypriot flag was positioned right in the centre of the hall. It felt like a good omen.

I was assigned to the red piste. As I stood there, I got goosebumps visualising myself fencing before the crowd. I was the sole competitor from Cyprus and my match would be broadcast live on national TV.

I had my schedule locked in: physical warm-up, treatment for my injuries from Maria, a fencing lesson with Ben and sparring with Raffi. Everything was in place. I was ready to go. I had my music playlist going and even brought a bag full of Cyprus T-shirts for Raffi to distribute to my supporters. Thirty minutes before the match, we went to the call room for equipment checks. Everything was set. We sat in pairs, waiting for our turn to head out to the piste.

Finally, it was time to perform. As we were walked down to the hall, I could hear the crowd building up behind the revolving doors. I shook Wojtowiak's hand and wished him luck. It was time to enjoy this moment.

The match

This match against Adrian Wojtowiak from Poland felt like a full-circle moment in my fencing career. His coach was none other than the coach of my very first coach. Here I was, 20 years later, fencing in the Olympic Games, a dream I'd had since I started fencing as a child. You couldn't have written it better.

When they called my name and I walked out onto the piste, it was magical. For fencers used to competing in quiet sports halls, the Grand Palais was majestic and grandiose. It reminded me of the Quidditch World Cup in Harry Potter, the seating just went up and up, filled to the brim with spectators. As I looked to the left, I saw the posters my sister had made, all the Cyprus flags and the T-shirts my supporters were wearing.

Tactically, I knew Wojtowiak would expect me to come out strong and aggressive. I was confident in my plan and believed I could execute it better than he could. We saluted, tested and the referees started the match. It began evenly with Wojtowiak scoring the first few points. It was clear he had done his homework and was trying to prevent me from dominating the bout. But soon, I found my rhythm and scored five points in a row, taking an 8–3 lead.

At that point, I felt like victory was within reach. But I made a critical mistake. My thinking momentarily switched from process to outcome. I rushed my actions, didn't prepare them well, and Wojtowiak capitalised on my errors, closing the gap to 8–7. My tactics were sound, but my execution faltered.

The match continued point for point until I regained control with some quick, well-executed attacks. Finally, I scored the last point to secure the victory. I had won a match at the Olympics. I shook Wojtowiak's hand, took a photo with Ben and looked across the hall to where my supporters were seated, chanting. Someone had told me to enjoy the experience no matter what and I took that to heart. I led them in a celebratory round of *olé*, relishing the moment of victory together.

Against the world number two

My next match wasn't for another 3½ hours. I had time to rest and prepare. In that moment, after feeling such pressure, I was grateful and proud to have won my first Olympic match. Now, with the world number two, Nick Itkin, as my next opponent, the pressure was off. If I lost but put up a good fight, people would pat me on the back and say well done.

Physically, the first match had been demanding: we scored a total of 25 points in under 80 seconds. I followed my recovery protocols: treatment, some food and then rest in the canteen area. Despite being at the Olympic Games, the most important competition of our lives, it just felt like another fencing competition while we were in the canteen.

We then started our tactical meeting for the match against Itkin. We agreed that if I used the same tactics I'd employed in the zonal competition and the match against Wojtowiak, I wouldn't stand a chance. Nick Itkin was world number two for a reason. He was incredibly strong in the middle of the piste and in defence. One key principle of his fencing was that he thrived in fast-paced bouts, feeding off his opponents' mistakes when they rushed at him.

To have any chance of winning, we decided I needed to slow the bout down, kill the distance, and push and pull him around the piste to draw out mistakes. From both a tactical and psychological standpoint, I had to take the match through at least two periods of fencing. The problem? None of my last ten elimination bouts had gone into a second period due to the aggressive tactics I'd been using. I had trained one way for nine months, but now I had to bring out plan B, a strategy that had been gathering dust. This was going to be a test of will and discipline. I'd have to call on all my experience and determination to make this work.

After going through my physio treatment, lesson and tactical analysis, I sparred with Raffi. He was mimicking Itkin's tactics and, honestly, he was destroying me. In jest, I had to ask him to let me win the last couple of points to boost my confidence.

When the organisers called us down, I could hear the crowd chanting. A couple of French fencers were fencing at the same time and the atmosphere was electric. One by one, we were introduced. As I stepped out onto the piste, I saw my supporters with their Cyprus flags, cheering for me. Just before I got into position, I looked up and around the Grand Palais. It was a truly magnificent venue.

I looked across at Nick Itkin as we saluted and got into position. The match began scrappily, going point for point. That was good for me. Being the superior technical fencer, Itkin excelled in clean, fast bouts, but I was bringing him down to a level that suited me. The score reached 4–4 and already 80 seconds had passed, the same amount of time it took to complete my first match of the day.

CONCLUSION

The plan was working, but then Itkin started to up the intensity in his attacks. He scored several quick points, bringing the score to 8–5 with a minute and 21 seconds left in the first period. I fought back and closed the gap to 7–8 and later to 10–12. Whenever I slowed the bout down and executed my attacks carefully, I scored. But if I rushed or was passive in defence, Itkin capitalised. At 10–12, I rushed my final attacks and wasn't disciplined enough, allowing Itkin to close out the match 15–10.

My Olympic competition was over. I couldn't have any regrets. I had given everything I possibly could in my preparation and on the day. I had gone toe to toe with one of the best fencers in the world and I had also become Cyprus' first-ever Olympic fencer to win a match.

After shaking hands with Itkin, his coach, the referees and Ben, I started to walk off quickly. Normally, I'm the first one out of there after a loss. But as I was leaving, I heard my supporters chanting, 'oh, Tofalides'. I stopped, turned around and clapped for them, appreciating their support. During the match, when I had scored a point to make it 8–10, I'd looked over at them and jokingly gestured for them to cheer louder, as their voices were being drowned out by the French crowd.

After the match, I gave interviews to Cypriot and Greek media, as well as the BBC World Service. It's always tough to give interviews right after a loss. You just want to get away, but it was important to share my thoughts with all those who had watched me compete back in Cyprus.

Then, I hugged Raffi, Maria and Ben, got changed and went to greet all the people who had come to support me. I gave a long, rambling speech, thanking everyone for their support over the years. Afterward, I packed my bags and headed back to the Olympic Village, knowing that tonight we would celebrate a day well fought and a journey well travelled.

On the way back, I felt physically and mentally exhausted. The adrenaline had worn off and fatigue was settling in. It was the first moment I had to reflect on the day's events. On the one hand, it was true, I had no regrets about my preparation or performance: I had given my all and I was proud of what I had achieved.

However, one thought lingered. Despite Itkin being ranked number two in the world, I genuinely believed I could have beaten him. After all, I had knocked out Olympic and world champions before. I knew anything could happen on any given day. The pressure of fencing in the zonal competition, where only one out of 30 fencers could qualify for the Olympics, had been the perfect training ground for managing stress at this level.

My only regret was that I fully believed I could beat him only once the match had already begun. It was the perfect set-up for an upset: I had already fenced a match in the round of 64, so I was familiar with the surroundings, the crowd and the protocols. I also didn't delve enough into Itkin's psychology. During the first couple of points, I could see he was nervous and flustered, even asking the referee to speak louder because he couldn't hear over the noise of the crowd. At 25, Itkin was six years my junior and newer to the fencing circuit, while I had the experience and mental toughness that came with age. The pressure was on him not to lose. I had nothing to lose and everything to gain.

In the end, I'd rate my performance as 8/10 for executing the tactics we had planned. But to win that match, I needed to be a 10/10. Itkin went on to win the bronze medal, but the experience left me thinking about what could have been.

CONCLUSION

That night, we had a dinner to celebrate followed by some dancing, a perfect way to cap off the day. The following day, I had one more opportunity to explore the Olympic Village. After the night out and the intensity of the fencing the day before, I was exhausted and didn't do much. We took it easy, enjoying what the Village had to offer and soaking up the last moments before heading home early the next morning.

I felt like we had truly made the most of this experience, not just for me but for my whole team. We had struck the right balance between enjoying ourselves and maintaining the professionalism needed to compete at this level.

Post-Olympic reflections and lessons

Reflecting on my Olympics, I can say with pride that it was a defining moment. After 21 years of dedication, training and competition, I finally achieved what had once seemed like a distant dream. While it will take me time to appreciate the magnitude of it all, what I take away from the experience goes beyond the personal. It is a deeper understanding of what it takes to excel at the highest level, not just in sport but in any endeavour.

Dreams

It's easy to underestimate the strength of having a clear, driving vision of where you want to go. For years, I dreamt of competing in the Olympics, visualising every detail, from stepping onto the piste to embracing my mother after achieving qualification. These visions were not merely motivational but essential. They kept me focused, resilient, and willing to push through the toughest challenges. Dreams, when paired with relentless belief, have the power to transform what feels impossible into reality.

Determination

Determination is the fuel that drives belief. I experienced countless moments of doubt, setbacks and frustrations: failing to qualify for the Olympics multiple times; injuries that sidelined me; and the pressures of balancing a career with personal commitments. But the one constant was my refusal to give up. Determination isn't just about persistence; it's about embracing the grind, pushing through the obstacles and never allowing defeat to define the end of your journey.

Adaptable

Life rarely goes as planned and the Olympics were no different. From injuries that required tactical changes to unexpected confrontations that threw off my focus, I learned that those who succeed aren't the ones who avoid challenges but those who face them head-on and adjust accordingly. Adaptation is not just a skill; it's a mindset that allows you to turn obstacles into opportunities.

Support

Behind every success story is a support network and mine was invaluable. From my coach, Ben, to my physio, Maria, and my family and friends who supported me unconditionally, their encouragement and expertise kept me grounded. Results are rarely achieved in isolation. Surrounding yourself with people who believe in you, challenge you and pick you up when you fall is vital. They help you become the best version of yourself and remind you of your strengths when you need it most.

Process

Performance isn't about moments of brilliance but the accumulation of perfected routines, habits and approaches. Whether it's a mental warm-up, strategic analysis or physical conditioning, mastering the small details day in and day out builds the foundation for big achievements. Perfecting these processes becomes a way of life, one that constantly evolves as you learn more about what works and what doesn't.

Compartmentalisation

In a world full of distractions and competing demands, the skill of compartmentalisation was a gamechanger for me. The ability to separate different parts of my life, focusing on one task at a time, was critical in balancing my training, work and personal life. Compartmentalisation doesn't just reduce stress. It increases the quality of your performance in each area of life. When I trained, I trained fully. When I planned my wedding or worked on my business, I gave that task my full attention. This skill allowed me to keep my head clear when it mattered most.

Learning

One of the most underrated skills in life is how quickly you can learn. The faster you can gather data, analyse it and adjust your approach, the more likely you are to succeed. Every loss, every setback is an opportunity to gain insight into yourself and your competition. The real winners are those who learn the quickest and apply that knowledge in real time. Fencing, like life, is a continuous process of learning, adapting and improving.

Circumstance

Outcomes are never entirely within our control. Circumstance and luck play a role too. I've seen incredible athletes falter through injury, timing or simply being in the wrong place at the wrong time. But luck, while out of our hands, is something you can prepare for. If you consistently put in the work, hone your skills and are ready for the opportunity, you give yourself the best chance of luck favouring you.

Self-awareness

In the end, what matters most is understanding yourself. No coach, no family member, no friend can take responsibility for your life. You alone are responsible for your successes and failures. It means knowing your strengths and weaknesses, learning from every experience and continuously refining your approach. Self-awareness is the key to unlocking your potential. Without it, you will always be at the mercy of external forces.

In life, we are given a limited time to make our mark. The reality is that 99.9 percent of people won't be remembered after their parents or grandparents. But that's not what matters. What matters is how you live the time you are given. Simply by being alive, you are lucky. So chase your goals, dream big and never give up. Life is short, but the impact you make in the pursuit of your dreams can last forever.

APPENDIX 1

ALEX'S FENCING CAREER

Year	Age	Event	Notes
2000	7	Started fencing	First picked up a sword at an after-school fencing club at University College School in London, UK
2005	12	Trained at Salle Paul, Highgate	Joined Salle Paul at William Ellis School, training under GB Olympic coach Ziemek Wojciechowski
2010	18	Youth Olympics, Singapore	Represented Great Britain at the inaugural Youth Olympics; inspired by the motto 'Dream it, believe it, achieve it'

2012	19	London Olympics	Narrowly missed selection for the four-man GB team; finished the season ranked 8th in the UK
2013	20	British champion	Became individual British senior champion
2014	21	World Championships	Qualified for first senior World Championships with Team GB; finished the season ranked 3rd in the UK
2015	22	Annus horribilis	My father and paternal grandparents all passed away in Cyprus within ten months
2015	22	European Games	Part of the Team GB squad that won team gold at the European Games in Baku, Azerbaijan
2016	23	Rio Olympics	Missed out on the four-man GB team for Rio 2016; ranked 5th in the UK that season

2017	24	Switch to Cyprus	Changed from Great Britain to represent Cyprus
2017	24	Results for Cyprus	Won a satellite world cup in Antalya, Turkey, at my first competition for Cyprus; placed 6th at the World Cup in Bonn
2021	28	Olympic qualifier, Madrid	Lost in the final of the European zonal qualifier for Tokyo 2021, narrowly missing the last ticket to the Olympic Games
26 April 2024	31	Olympic qualifier, Luxembourg	Won the European zonal qualifier, earning Cyprus its first Olympic fencing spot; culmination of a 21-year dream
July Aug 2024	31	Paris Olympics	Competed as Cyprus's first Olympic fencer at the Paris 2024 Games

APPENDIX 2

TERMS IN FENCING

Advance	A short forward step used to close distance.
Attack	The initial offensive action made by extending the arm and continuously threatening the opponent's target.
Beat attack	An attack that begins with a sharp tap on the opponent's blade to open a line.
Bout	A single match in fencing, contested to a set number of points or within a time limit.
Counterattack	An offensive action made in response to an opponent's attack, aiming to score before or during their movement.

Counterparry	A defensive blade movement that responds to an opponent's parry by reclosing the line.
Disengage	A blade movement that avoids the opponent's attempt to take the blade by moving in a small semicircle.
Distance	The physical space between fencers, manipulated to control timing and opportunity.
Double touch	In foil and sabre, a rare simultaneous hit; in épée, both fencers scoring at the same time.
Épée	One of the three fencing weapons. Entire body is valid target; no right of way rules apply; double hits are allowed.
Endgame	The closing phase of a bout where a small number of points remain, often requiring heightened focus.
Feint	A false attack designed to provoke a defensive reaction, creating an opening.
Fencing line	The imaginary vertical and horizontal divisions of target area that dictate where the attack is directed.

Fleche	A running attack where the fencer launches off their front foot to close distance quickly.
Foil	One of the three fencing weapons. Target area is the torso (front and back, but not arms, neck, or head); right of way rules apply.
Guard	The ready stance from which all actions begin, also referring to the protective part of the weapon's handle.
Lunge	The fundamental attacking action where the fencer pushes off the back leg, extending the front leg and arm to reach the opponent.
Parry	A defensive blade movement that deflects the opponent's attack.
Piste	The fencing strip, 14 metres long and 1.5–2 metres wide, where all official competition bouts take place.
Poule	A group stage in fencing competition where each fencer faces all others in the group.
Preparation	Movements made before an attack, such as footwork or blade work, to set up the action.

TERMS IN FENCING

Priority / right of way	The rule in foil and sabre determining which fencer is awarded the point when both land a hit.
Remise	An immediate continuation of an attack after the first action fails, without withdrawing the arm.
Riposte	An attack made immediately after successfully parrying the opponent's attack.
Sabre	One of the three fencing weapons. Target area is everything above the waist (excluding the hands); right of way rules apply. Hits may be made with the cutting edge or point.
Second intention	A tactical plan where the initial action is meant to draw a predictable response, which the fencer then exploits.
Stop hit	A counterattack made into the opponent's attack, attempting to land before their action completes.
Target area	The valid scoring zone in each weapon; in foil, it's the torso, including the back.
Tempo	The timing and rhythm of actions in fencing, manipulated to gain advantage.

Touch	A valid scoring hit in fencing.
Withdrawal / retreat	A backward step used to maintain or increase distance.
Zonal qualifier	A regional Olympic qualification tournament where only fencers from certain countries may compete.

APPENDIX 3

TERMS IN PERFORMANCE PSYCHOLOGY

Adaptability	The ability to adjust tactics, mindset or approach in response to changing conditions.
Attentional control	The skill of maintaining focus on the relevant cues while ignoring distractions.
Backwards planning	Preparing by starting with the end goal and working backwards to ensure all steps are aligned.
Belief	The conviction that you can succeed, even in high-pressure circumstances.
Champion's mindset	A combination of resilience, focus and discipline cultivated to compete at the highest level.

Clarity	A mental state where goals, priorities, and next steps are fully understood.
Compartmentalisation	Separating different tasks or emotions so that each can be dealt with fully and without interference.
Confidence building	Structured actions or routines that reinforce self-trust and readiness.
Emotional regulation	The ability to manage emotional responses under stress, keeping performance steady.
Endgame focus	The discipline to remain process-oriented when close to achieving a goal, avoiding distraction from the outcome.
Fight-or-flight response	The body's automatic physiological reaction to perceived threats, triggering heightened readiness to fight, flee or freeze.
Flow state	A mental condition of complete absorption in the task, often producing peak performance.
Goal setting	Establishing specific, measurable, achievable, relevant and time-bound objectives.

TERMS IN PERFORMANCE PSYCHOLOGY

Holistic effort	Applying maximum effort across all performance areas: physical, technical, tactical, psychological, nutritional, emotional and logistical.
Learning agility	The speed and effectiveness with which you can absorb lessons from experiences and apply them.
Mental warm-up	A pre-performance routine designed to optimise focus, confidence and readiness.
Narrative building	Creating and using empowering mental stories to direct focus and belief under pressure.
Pressure management	Strategies to stay calm, think clearly and execute effectively in high-stress moments.
Process focus	Concentrating on the steps and execution rather than the outcome.
Resilience	The capacity to recover quickly from difficulties and maintain performance standards.
Self-awareness	Understanding your strengths, weaknesses, habits and emotional triggers.

Self-mastery	The discipline to control thoughts, emotions and actions in pursuit of a goal.
Support network	The people whose encouragement, expertise and feedback enable sustained success.
Tactical mastery	The ability to analyse opponents, design winning strategies and adapt them in real time.
Visualisation	Using mental imagery to rehearse and reinforce performance.

APPENDIX 4

WORLD-CLASS MENTAL SKILLS IN FENCING

This framework was first developed in 2013, by Katie Warriner, performance psychologist to Team GB and co-founder of The Prime Clinic. Its purpose is to help athletes develop the mindset, skills, and habits to perform at their best and to thrive as people, on and off the piste.

It's built from shared experience of what it takes to excel, alongside evidence from performance psychology research. As fencers, Katie would always remind us:

> You are brilliantly unique, just like everyone else. We all have strengths and areas to develop. For some, the greatest performance impact comes from focusing on your strengths and keeping them in their sweet spot. For others, addressing areas of development is critical to unlocking performance. Use this framework as a source of inspiration and reflection, not a rulebook.

In elite sport, there are no guarantees. But excelling across these areas dramatically increases your chances of achieving your goals and doing so in a way that feels meaningful and sustainable.

How to use it

Rate yourself on each skill using a traffic-light system:

- **Red**: haven't yet developed this skill or quality.
- **Amber**: have some ability here, but inconsistent or incomplete.
- **Green**: strong, reliable skill that I can use consistently when it matters.
- **Gold**: truly world class, second nature and always there when I need it.

You're not being judged. It's about honest reflection and development. Share your self-assessment with your coach or trusted team-mates for feedback, then review regularly to track progress.

1. Raw ingredients

Ambition

- Clear dream or performance goal, including a vision for the kind of fencer you want to be.
- Strong personal reasons for wanting to achieve these dreams and goals.

- Inner drive to give your very best, whatever the outcome.

Commitment

- Understand the realities of the world-class journey: it's never guaranteed or smooth.
- Choose to give everything within my control to my goals.
- Build a well-informed, evidence-based plan, broken into achievable chunks, with timelines and strategies for overcoming obstacles.
- Fully believe in and commit to my plan.
- Anticipate likely challenges and prepare myself mentally.
- Keep professionalism high: doing what I said I'd do, having honest conversations, making smart performance choices.
- Manage life outside sport so it supports my ambitions.

Growth mindset

- Recognise the role of effort, learning and adaptability on the path to mastery.
- Welcome challenges and regularly push beyond comfort zones.
- Focus on my own improvement; see others as inspiration, not threat.
- Seek every opportunity to refine my performance, actively involving the right people (eg, coaches, physio, strength and conditioning, psychologist).

- Learn from setbacks: take appropriate responsibility, avoid blame, keep perspective.
- Open to feedback.

Confidence

- Know my strengths and celebrate them.
- Take ownership of success as well as learning from it.
- Draw on my strengths when it matters most.
- Able to keep my strengths in their sweet spot, not under or over play them.

Teamwork

- Understand that strong teams achieve more.
- Build the right support team around me.
- Communicate openly and respectfully.
- Give my team regular, honest and authentic feedback.
- Collaborate to solve problems and find opportunities.
- Express myself clearly and listen well.

Psychological awareness and enjoyment

- Understand the influence of the mind on performance.
- Recognise that mental skills can be developed through deliberate practice.

- Work on these skills consistently.
- Accept that not every moment will be fun, but able to enjoy the majority of the journey.
- Celebrate progress, effort and achievement, both big and small.
- Recognise that sustainable high performance isn't just about grit; it's also about rest, kindness to self and recovery.

Resilience

- Persevere through challenges, uncertainty and setbacks.
- Learn, adapt, and bounce back with renewed focus and determination.
- Build habits that allow me to switch off and recharge fully.

2. Training

Purpose-driven motivation

- Set clear goals for every session, linked to my long-term ambitions.
- See training as an opportunity to get better.
- Push myself to give my best effort every day.
- Train deliberately for pressure, not just assume skills will transfer.

Organisation and discipline

- Arrive prepared: on time, rested, fuelled, and equipped.

- Take care of my body (warm-up, cool-down, injury prevention).
- Commit fully to recovery and rehab plans.
- Manage tech, social media and distractions in ways that support focus, rest and wellbeing.

Learning mindset

- Review training regularly, alone and with your coach, to extract key lessons.
- Seek and apply constructive feedback.
- Track progress over time.

Managing emotions and distractions

- Recognise the difference between emotion and logic.
- Choose the mindset that best supports my performance.
- Manage stress effectively.
- Stay engaged from start to finish without letting emotions interfere with effort or quality.
- Manage relationships effectively, especially under pressure.

3. Competing

Perspective

- Maintain a healthy outlook; compete with confidence and enjoyment.

- Handle pressure and deliver my skills when it matters.
- Keep perspective after competitions, win or lose.

Game planning

- Collaborate with my coach to create clear, evidence-based plans built on my strengths.
- Be ready with plan B or C if needed.
- Build commitment to my plan through rehearsal and visualisation.
- Adapt game plans efficiently during competition.

Mindset on the piste

- Step onto the piste confident, composed and ready.
- Focus on process, not outcome, regardless of circumstances.
- Trust my training, skills and instincts under pressure.
- Access my full range of techniques and tactics when it counts.
- Commit 100 percent to every effort.

Focus and refocus

- Stay present: one hit at a time.
- Reset quickly after each point.
- Handle distractions like tough calls or opponent tactics with composure.
- Learn between fights, then move on positively.

Adaptability

- Adjust tactics decisively at the right moments.
- Stay receptive to coach input.
- Think clearly under fatigue and pressure.

4. Life and wellbeing

Balanced perspective

- Be clear on who I am beyond being a fencer.
- Know my core values and how they guide choices in and out of sport.
- Value myself as a person, regardless of results.
- Take responsibility for my choices.
- Maintain a positive outlook.

Support network

- Build and nurture strong relationships with family and friends.
- Stay engaged in life outside of fencing.
- Make time for activities that bring joy and recovery.

This framework is not a checklist to complete once: it's a living tool. Revisit it often, using it to guide honest reflection, focus training, celebrate progress and stay aligned with what matters most, not just in sport, but in life.

ACKNOWLEDGEMENTS

Firstly, my deepest thanks to my family. This book, and the journey it represents, would not have been possible without your love, patience and belief in me.

To my coaches past and present, thank you for shaping me not only as a fencer but as a person. From early lessons to the most crucial competitions, your guidance and trust have been invaluable.

To my support team at the Olympics and to those at Cyprus Fencing, British Fencing, the Cyprus Sports Organisation and the Cyprus Olympic Committee, your dedication behind the scenes made it possible for me to stand on the world stage.

The life of a fencer can sometimes feel lonely and selfish, but along the way I was never truly alone. I am grateful to all those who believed in me, trained beside me, analysed bouts with me and reminded me why I began this journey in the first place.

Finally, a message to fencers everywhere: this sport belongs to the world. The knowledge is out there and available to all. You do not have to come from a traditional fencing nation to achieve your dreams.

Find your own path and your own style of fencing. It is of course important to learn from others but if you imitate others, you will never be as good as them. Know your game well, your strengths and your weaknesses: mastering yourself is much more important than mastering your opponents. Finally, whether you are winning or losing, never give up.